Design Science Primer

Tools for Changing the World

Medard Gabel and David Heeney

First Edition

Designed by Mary Gabel, Gabel Graphics, Media, PA, www.gabelgraphics.com

ISBN-13: 978-1514365113
ISBN-10: 1514365111

Available at
www.designsciencelab.com
www.amazon.com

"The most important fact about Spaceship Earth: it didn't come with an operating manual."

—Buckminster Fuller

Dedication

This book would not be possible without the life and work of Buckminster Fuller. It is his insights, values, vision, and design initiatives that have informed and inspired the work found here.

Acknowledgements

The authors would like to acknowledge those who worked with Medard Gabel on an earlier version of this book, including Howard Brown, Robert Cook, Robert Blissmer, Geoffrey Hoare, Cathy Horvitz, Gail Ziegelmeier, and Jack Ren Marquette. That book, the *Environmental Design Science Primer*, now over thirty years old and seriously out of date, nevertheless served as an organizational inspiration for this document. The authors of this present volume thank those whose work inspired us.

CONTENTS

PART 1

PART 2

"When you're finished changing, you're finished."

—Benjamin Franklin

FORWARD

MODELS OF CHANGE/CHANGING THE WORLD

This book is about change.

   Behind every change is a theory of change. The theory answers the questions, "What is change? How do we understand it? How does change happen? How do we bring it about?" The following five pages show how we think change happens. This book is about how we bring it about.

   Everything that is shaping the world is brought about by various processes of change and their interactions. Processes, such as globalization, decentralization, democratization, technological innovation, economic development, evolution, design and planning, are drivers of change.

BigPicture CHANGE

Change is not a stand-alone event or singularity. It is a plural. Something always changes in relation to something else. It gets bigger, smaller, closer, older, better, easier, more complex, more numerous—relative to a reference point. We measure ourselves, our society, and most everything else, by how it and we change.

Change is what happens when the relationship between two or more entities shifts or transforms. Some forms of change are the result of large-scale natural and human generated processes. Some change is human generated.

Some aspects of change are seen as systematic and predictable, and others as random or coincidental. One form of the non-predictable changes are those that emerge from the accumulated interactions of parts. These emergent properties arise from the increasingly complex interactions of relatively simple parts. For example, the examination of a water molecule does not disclose a "surface" of the water. It is only when many water molecules are added together does a surface emerge.

Societal change is a highly complex process, involving many factors, such as demography, technology, availability of resources, politics, culture, needs, expectations, economics, and the interaction of these factors. Geography, access to resources, trade, openness to outside influences can have an impact on how a society changes, develops, or disintegrates.

> "In times of change, learners inherit the Earth, while the learned find themselves beautifully equipped to deal with a world that no longer exists."
>
> —Eric Hoffer

Living systems—social, economic, and political systems—change over time so they can stay the same—that is, so that they can maintain stability. The parts of all living systems are born, grow, reproduce, and eventually die. In this process, they change various aspects of themselves and the bigger system(s) of which they are a part. In turn, these larger systems change as they maintain the stability necessary for growth and evolution.

Human systems change because human beings change: they learn. Because it is difficult to impossible to learn less as we experience our lives (although many dogmas seek, at minimum, to freeze our learning at some convenient, understandable, or exploitable level), we learn more and more. And as we do so, we learn how to improve our surroundings and our lives. We learn how to do more with the resources we have access to. We learn how to improve our tools and organization so that they do more for us with the same or fewer resources. In short, we change. The purpose of which is to improve, while maintaining stability.

OurPicture CHANGE

The change we are most interested in here is the change that we bring about by our actions. Controlled or designed change is how we systematically change the world for the better. It is this type of change that this book if focused on. How do we bring about the changes we want? Or accelerate the ones we think are going in the right direction? How do we avoid the ones we don't want? Or reverse the ones going in the wrong direction? The science of design is the systematic process of changing something in a preferred direction. Like other sciences, it

> "Some people change the world by imposing their will on it. Some people change the world by discovering a truth. Some people change the world by changing people's minds. Some people change the world by creating things of great beauty. Some people change the world by making new tools for change."
>
> —Danny Hillis

formulates hypothesizes (Is it possible to provide clean abundant energy supplies in rural villages in the developing world?), tests these hypotheses (Will this solar panel provide enough energy in an affordable manner to meet the villages needs in a sustainable way?), and maximize what we can learn from our failures (Why didn't this configuration work as desired?)

The important thing about designed change is that it can be used by anyone to improve their world.

YOU CAN CHANGE THE WORLD

You can change the world. In fact you already have. Your mere existence has impacted the world in many ways: as a manufacturer of carbon dioxide and other by-products of your metabolism, as a consumer in the global and local economy, as a producer of some good or service for those same economies, as a parent, child, brother, sister, husband, wife— we have all impacted our homes, communities and by extension through the interconnections of globalization, we have impacted the world. That was the easy part.

SEVEN TECHNIQUES FOR CHANGING THE WORLD

But the above, "You can change the world" has a more dramatic, and important, meaning. You can also change the world volitionally. Not just through your passive presence in the world as a biological entity or part of an economic or family unit— you can, with intelligence, persistence, hard work, courage, initiative, and the synergy of "luck" that the previous qualities lay the groundwork for, change the world. That is, you can do something so innovative, so original, or so audacious, or so obviously right, or so sensible, or so perfectly matched to the needs of the time, that the world beats a path to your door and what you have done gets implement ed at a local and then global level, it gets replicated around the planet, and becomes part of the global culture.

You can change the world. There are ways that people have been doing exactly this for millennia. There are seven major techniques:

1 Evolution: The first and, up to now, the technique responsible for the most change, is evolution. Evolution is the slow change brought about by the long-term processes of nature selecting out the organisms and techniques and tools that lead to the most success over time of surviving.

2 Revolution: There are two major revolutionary pathways. One is relatively slow, lasting, and takes place in social, technological, and economic spheres. The other is faster, not necessarily long-lived, and takes place in the political arena.

a. Non-violent, knowledge-based revolutions, such as those based on knowledge and its applications as technology, such as the agricultural, industrial, and information revolutions, brought about widespread and profound change in all aspects of human life and well being.

b. Violent political or ideological revolutions, based on ideology and the use of weapons to overthrow or change political leadership, such as the American, French, Russian and Cuban revolutions brought about rapid political change.

3 Non-violent social action: Mahatma Gandhi and Martin Luther King, Jr. are examples of leaders of non-violent social movements of this kind. Whether passive resistance, economic boycotts or massive marches on political seats of power, this change mechanism has brought about huge changes in political and social realms. Another form of this form of change is the non-violent, orderly change that comes about in political structures, usually democracies, through voting and political decision making processes.

4 Scientific research: Who has more impact on the world, Karl Marx or the inventor of the telephone? Richard Nixon or Albert Einstein? Our increased understandings of how nature works, the scientific breakthroughs over time, have changed the world in more profound ways, and more rapidly and universally than almost any other technique.

5 Business and markets: In an age when everything is interconnected, the meeting of a need through a product innovation has the potential to change the world more rapidly than almost anything else in the past. Business can spread the advances of science as well as the ethical sensibilities of enlightened self-interest and concern and compassion for all the citizens of the world. It also has the option of ignoring these later considerations, focusing on just short- term gain, and harming environmental and social systems in which it is embedded.

6 Personal initiative: This, and perhaps the most important, technique incorporates elements from all the other techniques and leverages them to change the world. With the ex-ception of evolution, none of the above happen without individual initiative. Innovation is the key to nearly all of the change agents described above. Whether it is biological innovation brought about through natural evolution, or technological innovation brought about through industrial design processes, market pressures, or curiosity, innovation is the key.

7 Design Science: It couples the principles and findings of science with a moral vision of what should be and then takes ther personal initiative to develop solutions to real-world problems that can be implemented in markets and by governments, corporations, organizations, and individuals. It is based on individual initiative and uses market economies wherever possible and appropriate. It shares a concern for peace and social justice with those like Martin Luther King and Mahatma Gandhi, but uses technological and social innovation as change agents.

Innovation is the cause of change. New technology, new decisions, new ideas, new combinations of old systems bring about change. Whether it is the agricultural, industrial, in formation, or communication revolution, innovation was at the core of the changes. Someone found a new, and better, way of doing something that was previously being done, or they came up with a way of doing something brand new that no one was doing—but upon seeing it, most everyone immediately saw its benefits.

Innovation can be a variation of something already existing or a modification that improves quality or efficiency. It can be invention of something new. It can be a borrowing from another field, or diffusion from another geographical area. Many problems can be innovated out of existence. *This is what design science is all about—innovating basic human need problems out of existence.*

Some people change the world by making new tools for change. As a dramatic example of changing the world by making new tools, I include the creation of the Internet. I would also list something like building the rural credit system in Bangladesh as another example. Changing the world in this way can involve changing people's minds, and can entail imposing one's will to some extent, but it is mostly about enabling other people to change—by giving them tools to do so. This feels like progress. The other appeal of tool creating is that change brought about this way is self-sustaining and self-correcting. By self-sustaining, I mean you can use tools to make other new tools. This gives enabling tools a self-amplifying effect that can gain importance with time. I like that. I feel this is a very different way to change the world from trying to impose your will on it, because when you do that the world tends to snap back after you stop trying, or after you leave. Also, enabling change through tools is self-correcting. People who try to change the world by imposing their will on it often cause unintended harm, because the consequences of the change are hard to predict. When the beneficiaries control the change themselves, they have a lot more opportunity for feedback. Thus, change of this sort has a better chance of being good.

—Danny Hillis
Whole Earth Winter 2000

PART 1

CONCEPTUAL TOOLS/PERSPECTIVES

> **Part 1** Provides a big picture vision of change in which design projects and initiatives can be understood and conceived.

Change your perspective and you change the world.

Perspective is more important than IQ.

INTRODUCTION

Big Picture DESIGN

Everything is design.

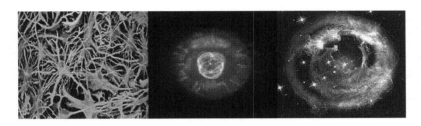

Whether it is the highway sign or the highway itself, the car you drive, the coffee cup you drink from, or your home, this book, the music you listen to, the movies you watch, or the language you use, *everything*—including you and the Universe itself—is design. Everything you can see, hear, touch, smell, or taste is a design, and has, in some form or another, "design specs." Everything you can apprehend or understand is because of the design of what something is.

The design could be in the blueprints, technical drawings, artist's vision, DNA, or the generalized principles of the cosmos, but design plays a crucial role: without design, nothing is.

Design is conceptual, weightless. It is information, organized by intelligence. Information, as design, determines what matter and energy can do. As such, it controls matter and energy. And because information,

as know-how (and know-what, and know-where, and why) is essentially unlimited—unlike our material and energy resources, it is the conceptual underpinning of the profoundly important claim and imperative that there is enough to go around on our limited planet to take care of everyone. Without the dramatically increased amount of know-how, compared with the stone age, for example, there is no way we could meet the basic human needs of the world's current population, nor those who will be added in the coming decades.

Why does this matter? As we will see, good design progressively substitutes information for matter and energy and does "more with less"—more strength, functionality, for longer periods of time, while using less materials and energy. As, for example, a high-strength metal alloy does more with less than its same weight non-alloy counterpart and allows us to build extraordinary things like jet engines, long bridges, and super sharp scalpels; or the latest micro chip that does more computations per second while using less energy than its predecessor, allowing ever more useful computers, mobile phones, and hybrid cars.

WHOLE TO PARTICULAR

Design is critical.

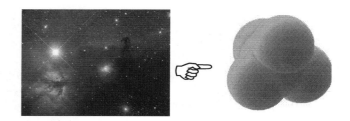

Design is critical to the survival and well being of the billions of people in the world. By one accounting, eighty percent of environmental impacts are determined at the design stage.[1] Given the above discussion, a case can be made that *all* environmental impacts are the result of design decisions.

All the products, services, and infrastructure that are meeting the needs of the world's population are the result of design. Some of this design is good, some shortsighted; a lot of it is unconscious, and even more the result of haphazard muddling through.

Whatever the problem or need, design plays an essential role in making the world work. Whatever the vision of how things should be, design plays an even more important role—which brings us to the reason for this book: If we are better at design, we will be better at meeting the needs of all the people of the world—and we will be better at making our vision of how things should be, real.

As the litany of problems the world faces transforms

Design: 1. To conceive in the mind; 2. to form a plan; 3. to have a goal or purpose; 4. a method for making, doing, or accomplishing; 5. the arrangement of resources to attain a preferred state.

Primer: 1. An elementary book for teaching children; any small book of elementary principles; 2. one who or that which primes; a cap, cylinder, etc. containing a compound which may be exploded by percussion or other means, used for firing a charge of powder. Prime mover: the initial agent that puts a machine in motion, as wind, electricity, etc.

from one crisis after another we are faced with an increasingly daunting challenge. Many would say these challenges are insurmountable and frightening. Others are convinced that human ingenuity is up to the task of saving itself. As H.G. Wells summarized over 70 years ago, *"Humanity is in a race between education and catastrophe."*

Whether it is climate change, hunger, terrorism, lack of health care, illiteracy, water shortages, environmental destruction, economic collapse, resource shortages, natural disasters, or poverty, the race is on. Can we make the world work for everyone, in a sustainable manner, before we run out of resources, destroy the environment's ability to regenerate itself, or the have-nots get fed up with the increasing gap between their children's prospects and those of the super-rich and take matters into their own hands—or the haves, afraid of losing what they have, do the same? In a well-armed and ever-increasingly better-informed world, where everyone knows how the other half lives, can the world afford to lose this race?

Will we be able to figure out how to meet the basic human needs of 100% of humanity in time? The technology and resources are available to feed, cloth, house, provide clean water, sanitation, energy, education, health care, communication, and transportation so that all of humanity has, at minimum, their basic human needs met. Given this, the challenge before us is fundamentally a design challenge: how do we design and redesign the world's life-support systems so that everyone is taken care of? How do we do this is a sustainable or regenerative way? And, how do we

> "How can we use science to help solve the daunting catalogue of trans-border health, energy and quality-of-life challenges confronting our globalized, 'flattened' world? By developing scientific and technological techniques that transcend disciplinary boundaries, reflect diverse perspectives, and incorporate the contributions of traditionally underrepresented groups."
>
> —Shirley Jackson, president of Rensselaer Polytechnic Institute

do this in as short a time as possible? That is what this book is about.

There are two major parts to this book. *Conceptual Tools* is primarily perspective, *Methodology* is a step-by-step process for doing design and strategic planning for the improvement of the world.

DESIGN SCIENCE IS . . .

Design Science is a methodology for changing the world. It involves the application of the principles and latest findings of science to the creative design and implementation of solutions to the problems of society.

It is a way of recognizing, defining, and solving complex problems that is based on innovation and thrives on transparency. It takes a whole systems, global, and anticipatory approach that fosters creative collaboration and synergy in the development of comprehensive solutions to both global and local problems. It was inspired by the work of Buckminster Fuller and other planners, scientists, and visionaries.

How is Design Science Different from Other Planning Processes?

Unlike many planning and political processes that compartmentalize issues and seek to develop solutions in a vacuum, Design Science stresses comprehensive thinking based on a clear understanding of the state of the world, available resources, appropriate technology, culture, environmental constraints, and the interconnections between world problems and opportunities. The Design Science planning process provides a framework for devising solutions to current problems as well as anticipating future needs.

Design Science is different from other problem solving and planning methodologies in its comprehensive, anticipatory, inclusive, and transparent approaches to the development of solutions. It takes a 'whole to particular' approach that is both global in perspective and in its examination of options. It seeks to build capacity rather than merely solve problems, and to develop solutions that are transformative rather than merely the reforming of already inadequate systems. It is informed by a moral vision that places a priority on designing ways of meeting unmet basic human needs in ways that are environmentally sustainable and socially just.

The core of this approach to problem solving and planning is both a concern with whole systems—the whole Earth, the entire history of the planet, the global economy, all of technology, and all of humanity; both those living now and those yet to be born—as well as a recognition that everything is implemented locally, and that the "whole" is merely the context for the local. Design science has both a global perspective and a local focus. It is the local upon which the success or failure of a particular design solution will thrive or die.

Design Science is *comprehensive*, in that it starts from the whole system and works back to the special case. It deals with all facets of a problem including the larger system of which the problem is a part; in this sense, design science seeks to build capacity, not just solve problems. It is *anticipatory*, in that it seeks to recognize the threats coming down the pike before they arrive full blown on an unsuspecting or ill-prepared society; and it deals with the way things are going to be when the solution is going to be implemented, not just the way things are in the present. It is a *design* strategy, in contradistinction to a political or 'let's pass-a-law-and-change-human-behavior' approach; it seeks to change the larger system of which the specific problem is a part through the introduction of innovative artifacts or policies. It is a *science* in that it seeks to use evidence based solutions rather that politics, ideology, or wishful thinking to solve problems. Its definitions of problems and their solutions is science based, but relies more on synthesis than reductionistic thinking. (Describing design science through the paradigm of science, you can say that design science seeks to formulate its designs and problem solutions as testable hypothesis. A design prototype is an experiment to test the hypothesis. If the hypothesis, after testing is "true", the prototype can be scaled up and go into mass production.)

This *"comprehensive anticipatory design science"* is at least as much a perspective on the problems of the world as it is a methodology for tackling those problems. When applied to contemporary problems, it can lead to strikingly fresh insights and solutions.

Design science is a tool that is based on a global perspective and a systems approach to the problems of the world. It assumes that globalization has made the world an ever more interconnected whole, and any successful problem solving of society's systemic ills needs to be an approach that is global, comprehensive, visionary, and based on science, not politics, ideology, or wishful thinking. The entire world is now the relevant unit of analysis, not the city, state, or nation. At the same time, design science is also locally focused on specific conditions, climate, culture, capacities, resources, and needs. It is not a top-down approach to problem solving, nor is it a typical "bottoms up" approach. Design science combines global perspectives with a local focus that meets between the reality of specific need and global capacity. It seeks to harness the capacity and breadth of global options to the needs of a specific person, home, village, city, or region.

We are onboard, as Buckminster Fuller pointed out, "Spaceship Earth," and the illogic of 200+ nation state admirals all trying to steer the spaceship in different directions is made clear through this metaphor—as well in Fuller's more caustic assessment of nation states tending to act as "blood clots" in the world's global metabolism. And just as the Spaceship is, in fact, on one trajectory around the Sun, all the many billions of individuals aboard that ship have their unique and diverse paths and needs. Recognizing that the macro and micro are not mutually exclusive, but are two sides of the same problem solving coin, is an essential skill of design science.

The design science process is augmented by vast quantities of statistical information about the state of the world, its resources, human trends, needs, and technology. With the advent of personal computers and the Internet this information became almost universally available—and as it did so, design science can be undertaken by vastly more people. Coupled with the tools of the information age, design science gains the power to reach its potential. The Internet has not leveled the global playing field so much as expanded it, and the good-ol'-boy-status-quo-maintaining political process can now be subverted by a process that brings Thomas Jefferson's notions of egalitarianism into the twenty-first century.

Design science is not another specialized discipline but rather an integration of disciplines. Its practice is not a further winnowing out of the secrets of the universe, as in research at the frontiers of physics or biology, but an integrative discipline wherein the findings of the sciences and humanities are brought to bear to solve humanity's problems.

In Fuller's words, design science is a process where individuals or teams of people can "make the world work, for 100% of humanity, in the shortest possible time, through spontaneous cooperation, without ecological offense or the disadvantage of anyone."

Making the world work for 100% of humanity reflects Fuller's global perspective as well as his values. We are not here just to make ourselves rich, famous, or top consumer of the day or decade, or here just for the 5% living in our part of the world; we are here for all humanity. The "spontaneous cooperation" in the above quote is instructive in light of the previous discussion. The phrase does not read, "make the world work for 100% of humanity through a central government, through enforced coercion by a strong military, or the dominant superpower" but through a cooperation that arises from a fundamental transparency of society and its needs. If everyone knows what the situation is, has a clear vision of what should be and what needs to be done, we cooperate to get it done—as we do as a society in times of emergency.

Fuller said: *"I am enthusiastic over humanity's extraordinary and sometimes very timely ingenuities. If you are in a shipwreck and all the boats are gone, a piano top buoyant enough to keep you afloat that comes along makes a fortuitous life preserver. But this is not to say that the best way to design a life preserver is in the form of a piano top. I think that we are clinging to a great many piano tops in accepting yesterday's fortuitous contrivings as constituting the only means for solving a given problem."*

Design science is a method for developing the life preserving and enhancing solutions to society's problems. It is a method of doing away with the fortuitous contrivings of society and replacing them with designed solutions that are regenerative, affordable, and increase the well being of the whole world.

Design SCIENCE is

Proactive: In contradistinction to reactive and inactive planning, design science assumes the future is controllable. Life depends less on what happens than what we do. Design science is concerned with developing a vision of a desirable future and the ways of bringing it about. It is concerned more with designing the future than forecasting it, and the idealization of a system rather than it optimization. Design science is motivated by aspiration rather than fear.[2]

"Most current efforts to improve society are directed at getting rid of what we do not want rather than getting what we do want. Getting rid of what we do not want often results in getting something worse."

—Russell Ackoff

Local Band-Aids on systemic problems do not help anyone but Band-Aid manufacturers.

PRESENT DAY PROBLEM SOLVING

Present day problem solving and planning is the attempt to solve 10 to 20 year regional or global problems with 2 to 4 year local solutions staffed by bureaucrats with 1 to 2 year appointments funded with 1 year allocations that have been budgeted by politicians who can't see further ahead than 6 months, the next vacation, or next election (which ever comes first), who know next to nothing about the problem they are addressing, other than it does not, like bell bottom pants and lava lamps, seem to go away if ignored, and who were elected by voters informed by sound bites and situation comedies, and who see adversity as an excuse to go shopping. The best that we can expect from this process is that which will fail slowly. We are trying to solve vast problems with half-vast solutions. Or, as Mark Twain said, *"Sometimes I wonder whether the world is being run by smart people who are putting us on or by imbeciles who really mean it."*

Present day problem solving and planning is usually one of two types:

1. **Reactive planning:** This form of problem solving tries to undo what has been done. It seeks to prevent real change. It is orientated towards threats rather than opportunities; it repairs faults in the present rather than prepares for the future. Reactive planning usually seeks to find someone to blame; it looks for a simple thing and then removes it, Its normal mode is repression or elimination; science and technology are often seen as the villain. Reactive planning is motivated by fear. Its solutions are often human orientated—the problem solver finds out who the troublemaker is and gets rid of him. This form of planning sees the world as a series of machines.

2. **Inactive planning:** This form of problem solving sees the current situation is OK—and if nothing is done, things will stay the same. Their motto is "Do nothing and nothing will change." Inactive planning seeks equilibrium, to keep things the way they are. This form of planning is characterized by people who are busy as hell doing nothing. There is an abundance of red tape, bureaucracy, committees, and elaborate rituals that give the impression of something being done. There is a paralysis of analysis, and a hesitancy that borders on inability, to act.

Present day problem solving and planning characterized by:
* *Overspecialization, reductionism, local focus hocus pocus*
  Attempting to solve complex, interlinked global and local problems with simple solutions is like rearranging the chairs on the deck of the Titanic.

- *Scarcity/zero-sum dementia*
  Attempting to solve complex, interlinked global and local problems while assuming there isn't enough to go around guarantees that there will not be enough to go around.
- *Crisis-to-crisis management, reactive problem solving*
  Attempting to solve complex, interlinked global and local problems while the ship is smashing into an iceberg is neither productive or healthy.
- *Obesiodity; more of more*
  Attempting to solve complex, interlinked global and local problems with more of the same is like increasing the speed of the Titanic as the solution to the iceberg.
- *Mechanistic models*
  Attempting to deal with living systems with mechanical models guarantees solutions that are dead in the water.
- *Top down*
  Attempting to solve complex, interlinked global and local problems without the input, cooperation and creative involvement of those who will benefit from the solution produces dull exercises in futility (or exciting, but deadly, voyages on "unsinkable" ships).
- *Ideology*
  Attempting to solve complex, interlinked global and local problems with ideology is like believing your ship is unsinkable.

PLANNING VS. DESIGN SCIENCE

ASPECTS	PRESENT PLANNING	DESIGN SCIENCE
Area of focus	Local	Global *and* local in global context
Time horizon	Short range	Long range
Response	Emergency/crisis to crisis/ reactive	Anticipatory/ proactive/ initiative
Models	Mechanistic	Biological
Methodology	Reductionism/ specialized	Synthesis/ Comprehensive
Resources	Assumes scarcity	Assumes enough for all/abundance
Approach	"Solves" problems; reactive or inactive	Builds capacity; proactive
Environment	Non-sustainable	Regenerative
Solutions	Laws that seeks to change man	Artifacts that change the environment
Political framework	Top down	Network
Social role	Status Quo	Change Makers
Business approach	Manager	Entrepreneur
Problem approach	Reformation	Transformation

CONCEPTUAL TOOLS OF DESIGN SCIENCE

*"*Humanity on Earth teeters on the threshold of revolution. It has to be success for all or none. If the revolution is a bloody one, humanity is through. The alternative is a design-science revolution.*"*

—Buckminster Fuller

A conceptual tool is a concept used for patterning thoughts; it is often a metaphor that organizes information. For example, the metaphor "Spaceship Earth" organizes our perceptions about our environment in an entirely different way than just the word "earth." The conceptual tool is a method for organizing information, thought and eventually behavior.

The following conceptual tools have been found to be effective for organizing, explaining, and predicting various facets of our information environment in ways that lead to effective solutions to global and local problems. The design scientist uses these tools to elucidate relationships among existing information and to help produce new information. These conceptual tools should be viewed as a set of interrelated concepts to be used as a whole.

1. Think in SYSTEMS

Thinking in systems helps us recognize, define, and solve problems. Everything we can describe is a system because anything we can identify is, by nature, composed of a plurality of components. The Earth is a system, you are a system, and I am a system. What we design is a system. So what are systems? Here are their characteristics:

- A system is a whole. It has parts that interact and a boundary that divides it from the outside world.
- It is a set of two or more interrelated elements that can be subdivided into parts.
- The parts of a system interact in ways such that the behavior of the whole system is unpredictable if you look at just the behavior of the parts.

- A system's boundary divides the world into everything that is inside the system and everything that is outside the system. Changes often occur at the boundaries— where a system comes in contact with other systems of which it is a part, and its environment.
- A system is a stable organization of interacting parts. Systems change to maintain dynamic equilibrium.
- Systems are goal-seeking, having their own agenda based on the interaction of their parts. This agenda is seldom, if ever, completely understood, especially by the parts of the system.
- Systems have delays and time lags between an action, reaction, and resultant.
- You cannot change just one thing in a system. As a stable pattern of interacting parts, everything in a system is interconnected.
- Systems modify their environments, which in turn, modify the system (this can sometimes be seen as

"every solution creates new problems).

- The more a system can change the better able it is able to survive and thrive.
- Some systems change cyclically. Some change is transformative. Transformative change is change to new levels. This is often called "phase change."
- Is a system is not allowed to change non-violently, it will change violently. (Wars are a systems response to inflexibility or inability to change in non-violent ways.)
- Systems have feedback, both positive and negative
- Systems self-organize
- Living systems are self-maintaining, repairing and replicating.
- All living systems are made of matter and energy organized by information. The human body is a complex system comprised of less complex systems (nervous, circulatory, digestive, muscle/skeletal, etc. systems), organs (heart, stomach, etc.), cells, molecules, and atoms.
- All systems, whether ecological, technological, social, or conceptual have an environment into which they fit.
- Systems follow general rules or "laws" that help in explaining present behaviors and predicting future ones.

Being able to clearly understand relationships between a system and its environment is crucial because systems are always affected by their environment. (There are a number of tools that help us clarify a system's interactions with its environment. These are listed in the Methodology section of this document.)

Why Think in Systems?

Thinking in systems means that the designer/problem solver/strategic planner sees the world as interacting units that follow certain general patterns of interaction.

Systems thinking helps the problem solver see the world at a level of detail that is not so complex that any action is hopelessly mired in such minute detail that cause and effect is undetectable, nor so simplistic that any suggested action is unrelated to a measurable impact. Systems help the problem solver recognize cause and effect, action and impact, and general patterns of development. But this only works if the analysis is on a consistent *level of aggregation*.[3] It does not work if the systems being related are on, for example, the molecular level and that of social systems.

Some useful general rules or patterns of systems include:

The law of whole systems/synergy

"Synergy" (the behavior of the whole is unpredictable by the behavior of the parts taken separately; or more simplistically—the whole is greater than the sum of its parts), is embodied in the very definition of a system. It's corollary, "the known behaviors of the whole system and the known behaviors of some of its parts makes it possible to discover or to predict the behavior of the remainder of the system's parts" can be a useful tool in design science. For example, knowing the behavior of what the preferred energy (or other system) is helps the designer decipher the behaviors of the parts of that system. (For more on this, see "Preferred State Envisioning" in the *Methodology* section.)

Another facet of the principle of synergy is the property of *emergence* in complex systems. When systems (materials, people, artifacts, etc.) interact there arise new properties that result from the relation of one system to another. This emergence of new properties from the relationships of the parts and their interactions with their environment underlies much of design science and the scaling of solutions to meet global problems.

The law of requisite variety/redundancy ensures survival

Originally formulated in the field of cybernetics, this general rule says that the larger the variety of actions available to a system, the larger the variety of perturbations it is able to adapt to. Or stated another way: a flexible system with many options is better able to cope with change. A system that is tightly optimized for an initial set of conditions might be more efficient while those conditions prevail but fail totally should conditions change. And in today's world, conditions change constantly. For the design scientist this means that the more flexible the design, the more staying power it has.[4]

2. Start with the WHOLE

In order to maximize the odds of success, any problem-solving endeavor should start with the "whole" and work towards the particular. In this way, there is an increased probability of not leaving out critical variables. (Given the above dictum, "The only way to understand a system is to understand the system of which it is a part" by including the larger system, your analysis of the problem will not leave out important parts.)

There are many conceptual "wholes" from which to begin subdividing. For example, the universe, the Earth, all of humanity, all of humanity's problems, all the interlinked systems of life support, all the variables of a particular problem, all of the resources of the Earth, the entire history of the problem or systems being studied, and the preferred functioning of the system being designed. In general, the larger the system with which you start problem definition and alternative inventory, the more complete will be your work. Practically, problem analysis should begin at least two levels above the assumed level of the problem system. One of the rationales of this "starting with the whole" is that by doing so the designer has a higher probability of dealing actual causes, rather than just symptoms of problems.

> "If a problem can't be solved as it is, enlarge it."
> —Dwight Eisenhower

As indicated above, the "Law of Whole Systems" suggests that by putting together what is known about the whole with what is known about some of its parts, it is possible to progressively understand more about unknown parts. Since "problems" are parts of larger systems, we can solve a single problem only by understanding its relationship to other problems and to the larger environment.

Local problems should be viewed in the context of global problems for at least three reasons: first so that seemingly unpredictable aspects of the local system(s) can be better understood by the behavior of the larger system of which they are a part; second, so that more options—those contained in the larger systems—are available to the problem solver; and third, so that implemented local solutions don't create problems elsewhere in the larger system.

Spaceship Earth

Earth is a small automated, spherical spaceship orbiting at 67,000 miles per hour (108,000 km/h) around the Sun, which in turn is on its own course at 135 miles per second within the galactic nebula.[5] With the exceptions of radiation from the Sun and the gravitational effects of the Moon on oceans and atmosphere, the Earth can be viewed as a relatively closed system.

The conception of Earth as a spaceship helps us to organize our thinking about ourselves. The metaphor can help to make us aware that we are inherently linked to the well-being and effective operation of this tiny ship; like astronauts, we are responsible for the maintenance of the craft that protects and supports our lives. The metaphor is *not* intended to suggest that the Earth is a simple machine, or to diminish its beauty or integrity—or to suggest that it is only here for humans.

The idea that humanity is responsible for its action is fundamental to design science. Since Spaceship Earth did not come with an operating manual, our future depends on our ability to learn and to employ our knowledge in designing the best possible solutions to our problems. The Earth is a "whole" from which to begin a systematic design science process.

The Whole World Is Now the Only Relevant Unit of Problem Solving.

Globalization has, whether we like it or not, made us all one. We have always been voyaging on one ship, the SS *Earth*, but globalization has transformed this philosophy into an economic, technological, political, and ecological reality that is unavoidable, no matter how high the walls on our gated community or how far removed from the centers of civilization we choose, or are forced, to live.

A global approach is not altruism, some noble gesture by the rich to help out the less fortunate; it is a self-serving, pragmatic economic strategy. It is not much of a leap to see the enormous implications of adding an additional three to four billion consumers to the global economy. In a regenerative system, when these new "middle class" people leave poverty behind and join the global economy, they don't deplete the world's capacity, they add to it.

Moreover, the most cost-effective solutions are now global ones. For example, it makes no sense to try to eliminate deadly or debilitating diseases from just the U.S. or Europe if we do not also eliminate them from the rest of the world. The economics (to say nothing of the ethics) are compelling: for example, since smallpox has been eradicated from North America and Western Europe, those regions have saved over $5 billion on what they were spending each year on smallpox control within their borders (vaccination, border monitoring, etc.)

Metaphors come with strings attached

The metaphor "lifeboat," when used to describe the condition of the world, (as in "lifeboat ethic") suggests that if the lifeboat is seamingly "filled" then it is necessary to keep those in the water out of the lifeboat, or else one risks capsizing the boat, and all are lost. Seeing the world as a spaceship, rather than a lifeboat, means that if there is a leak in the starboard side, we all go down. One metaphor is a rationalization for genocide, the other for seeing how everyone's fates are intertwined and for making sure everyone survives.

More than 40 million cases of smallpox in the world have been avoided since its eradication.[6] If each of these cases caused a mere $1,000 in economic loss, that translates into a savings of $40 billion to the global economy—more than 130 times the original investment of $300 million.[7] A global approach will produce cost-effective solutions to all our basic problems of human need, environmental threats, and security—not just disease eradication.

Another example of self-interest is even closer to home: It is not too difficult, in a post-9/11 world, to point out to Americans and other citizens of wealthy nations the advantages of a world free of the festering poverty that underlies resentment towards conspicuous consumption in a world of haves, have-nots, and have-no-hopes. On a fundamental level, as the desperately poor get their needs met, the entire world becomes more secure, stable and safe for everyone. Wealth is a function not only of how much you have, but also of where you have it. If you have $10 billion of gold bullion on a sinking luxury liner, you are just going to sink faster. Making the world work for 100 percent of humanity means that wherever we are and no matter how rich we are today, we will then be even "richer"—more secure, safe, and in an almost infinitely more rich and stimulating cultural environment.

> Russell Ackoff has said, "When architects design a house, they begin with a sketch of the whole, not of each room." I think it can also be said that before the architect begins to sketch he or she has both an understanding of what the needs of the client are, and a vision of what would meet or surpass those needs.

3. Think LONG TERM

> "If you cannot draw on 3000 years of history, you are living hand-to-mouth."
> —Goethe

Design science operates in a long-term framework—not next quarter's profit margin, next year's election, nor even the next generation. It seeks to develop solutions in ways that a problem transforms into additional capacity. Not only is the next generation taken care of, so are all succeeding generations.

A short temporal focus is analogous to a small spatial focus: both are ineffectual, costly, counter-productive, and more than likely destructive to the well being of the whole system. Whether that system is your body and the short-term focus your fondness for fatty foods and the couch near the TV, or society's fixation on political platitudes like "no child left behind" that provide an illusion of educational reform—the short term is often at odds with the well-being of the whole over the long term. Investments in renewable energy, affordable health care, and universal education are positive examples of how a view to the long term can help

Global Timeline:
5 Billion Years

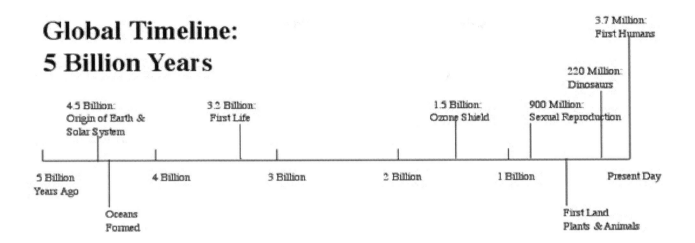

out in the short term. This is not to say that a concern with next quarter's profit is foolish, only that next quarter needs to be in tune with the next ten to twenty years. The larger the temporal frame of reference, the more possibilities there are and the deeper is our understanding of the past and its implications for the future.

In addition, looking at the world through the long-term lens makes prevention, rather than treatment or cure, the logical and most economical option. For example, a focus on the short term led the U.S. to provide $4 million a year in aid to boost agricultural productivity in Ethiopia. In 2003 when crops failed and famine threatened, the U.S. was compelled to send in $500 million in emergency food aid.[8] Another example of a short range, "least-cost" strategy that backfired was the U.S. approach to dealing with AIDS in Africa. The U.S provided about $50 million a year to Africa for AIDS prevention in the 1990s. By 2004, with over 20 million dead and another

> "A politician is a man who thinks of the next election; while the statesman thinks of the next generation."
>
> —James Freeman Clarke

30 million infected, the U.S. is now spending $3 billion per year to treat the disease.[9]

A long-term focus is helpful from another perspective as well. When viewed from the long term, most everything can be seen to be part of a process that has a *gestation rate*. All living systems, from human babies (9 months) to elephants (21 months) to motor vehicles (4 to 6 years) and computers (12 to 18 months) have their own unique gestation rate. Design science solutions to problems need to be aware of these varying rates of gestation. It also helps to realize that no matter how much you might like the world to change overnight, there are some processes that can not be rushed without the risk of a still birth.

Another conceptual spin-off of a long-term focus is that *everyone is needed*. The bigger the picture the designer has, the more important becomes the input and buy-in of all the stakeholders in a given design solution. The old way (characterized (chariture) above as "current planning techniques") dictated that to build a bridge you needed an engineer. Building a bridge today, we need the engineer but also the people who are going to use that bridge; those who are going to build it, manufacture the parts, and obtain the raw materials; the ecologists who will tell you where it can be placed so that it does the least damage to the environment; and most important, the citizens who will decide if they want the bridge in the first place and who will pay for it, in one way or another.

This is not neo-liberal do-gooder public policy rhetoric; it is pragmatic, cost-effective essentials for regenerative development. The day of the "expert" is over. Or more precisely, the day of the technological expert riding roughshod over culture, ecology, and values is over. Everyone is an expert on what they want and know. Further, the expert's education and experience is a double-edged sword. On the one hand it helps him or her to see opportunities to apply solutions that worked in other contexts. On the other, it may blind him or her to novel solutions.

The discussion table needs to include all stakeholders, or the capacity building that is critical to any endeavor will not reach its potential. The nation state is no longer the only major player on the global stage. Global corporations, cities, nations, NGOs, and private citizens all need to work together on getting what the world wants.

If the "problem" being addressed is to be solved (and stay solved), decision making at the local level and input from all sectors of local society are needed. This provides learning and growth opportunities for the larger system of which the problem is a part. Every development strategy is an opportunity to increase the knowledge and capacity of the society in which development is occurring.

> "We are made wise not by recollecions of the past, but by our responsibility to the future."
> —Gm B. Shaw

4. Technology as a LIVING SYSTEM

Biology Replaces Mechanics

The models we use shape the way we see the world and our reality. Using mechanistic models for problems has led the world to mechanistic solutions—solutions that fail when one of the cogs in the machine fails, that are seen as "independent" of their environment, and that regularly create as many new problems as old ones they solve. Viewing the world as a living system fosters a respect for a problem's complexity, an awareness of the context or environment in which it is embedded, and the possible solutions that can result in strengthening the health of the system and the elimination of the problem.

Viewing our technology as a collection of independent machines, each composed of myriad parts, none of which are related, all of which somehow add up to a life-support system for humanity is, in the end, a debilitating and lifeless view of technology and our role in creating that technology. Seeing our technological systems as living systems, interrelated and interdependent as the various systems and components of our own bodies and their environment, even going so far as to see technology as biology, leads to a whole new perspective on everything from the historical developments (embryology) of technology, possible options that mimic nature and living systems (biomimicry), to current and future trends (teleology), and even for the philosophically minded, humanity's role in the universe (cosmology). Seeing our collective life-support system as an *external metabolic system*, analogous to, but more differentiated than, our individual life support system we refer to as our internal metabolic system, helps us realize the interrelatedness of all our technology, it's multiple functions in society, and it's vital role in maintaining our viability as a species. Most importantly, given the present state of our ignorance about our environmental interactions, it helps us to see the vital connections between our living systems and our environment. Viewing our technology as an external metabolic system, the healthy functioning of which is essential for humanity's health and well being, makes the notion of "zero emissions" not just a utopian fantasy or environmental platitude but as important as stopping the internal bleeding of a wound to an individual human being.

As we create tools, we recreate ourselves

Using biological models leads to the use of biological or ecosystem based management tools. Such big picture management helps put the value of our environmental resources in a context that illustrate their true value. It leads to the reversal of management priorities—putting the value of the environment first and the target of

FUNCTION	INTERNAL METABOLICS	EXTERNAL METABOLICS
Distribution of utilizable resources to specific receptors	Circulatory system	Transportation system
Distribution of utilizable resources to specific receptorsntegrate, regulate whole system functioning	Central Nervous system, Endocrine system	People, Government, Media, Communications systems
Organize utilizable matter/ energy configurations into forms for action on the environment	Muscle, Skeletal, Integumentary systems	Motors, Tool-Making Industry, Manufacturing Industries
Convert matter/energy configurations to utilizable forms or dispose of them	Digestive, Excretory systems	Smelting and Refining, Materials conversion Industry, Waste Disposal/ Recycling Industries
Convert matter/ energy configurations into utilizable energy sources	Respiratory system	Power conversion technology
Protection from outside/ environmental forces	Skin	Shelter

exploitation (fish, food, forest, minerals), second.[10] In information short or uncertain circumstances it provides a logic for erring on the side of caution when setting production quotas or targets. It also helps shift the burden of proof so that economic production does not take place unless it can be shown that it does not harm or lower the value of the environment.

We can view technology as an externalization of the functions performed by the human body. As our early cousins needed something sharper than fingernails, they developed the sharp stick, rock, and eventually metal knife. As they needed something harder than a fist, they developed the wooden club, the rock hammer, and eventually the metal hammer. The clay cup developed from their needs to hold water—and eventually other liquids—hot, cold, acidic, boiling, melted, cooking—and in quantities our cupped hands could not handle.

Seen this way, all technology owes its origins to original functions performed for primitive society by our bodies. Tools and technology become extensions of what our bodies originally did. Once externalized, the former "simple" function of our bodies took on a number of extra-ordinary characteristics. For one, it could be "mass produced" so that hundreds of others could use my hands for holding water. Two, once externalized, the function my cupped hands preformed could be enlarged so that large quantities of liquids, or solids, could be contained. The externalized "hands" could also now be safely put in the fire or hold things for long periods of time without leaking. I could even make this container or vessel so large that it would not only be no longer recognizable as the externalization of the function my cupped hands preformed, but so large that I could get into this vessel and take it to the other side of the lake. Most importantly, when technology is seen from this perspective, it is no longer random chaos, or merely the stuff that pollutes the world and puts people out of work. Seen as a living system that follows the general rules of all living systems, technology becomes more understandable, predictable, and "friendly." Viewing technology as a living system provides insight into the interdependence of all the components and processes of our technological systems

Just as internal metabolics is the life-support system of our bodies and individual consciousness, external metabolics is the life-support system of collective humanity.

5. MORE with Less

"More with less" refers to the systematic process of substituting information for materials and energy. Weightless information, in the form of increased understanding and knowledge, is substituted for weighable materials and energy in such ways that the efficiency of the system is increased. "Efficiency" being defined as increased performance per each gram of materials and erg of energy used.

Getting ever-higher performance out of every gram of material and erg of energy invested in every function performed by our human-made life-support is critical to making the world's limited resources meet what appear to be the unlimited needs of our growing population and to reducing our impact on our environment. The concept of doing "more with less" also furnishes the design scientist with a standard by which strategies and solutions may be evaluated.

Buckminster Fuller pointed out that the sum total of the world's technology was operating at around 4 percent efficiency in the 1960s.[11] More up-to-date analysis has put the efficiency of the U.S. economy at around 6 percent.[12] By raising the efficiency of how we manufacture, use, and dispose of our products, we could raise the overall efficiency of our technological life-support systems four-fold.[13] Many products can be made five, ten, even one hundred times more efficient in their use of materials and energy.[14]

Examples of more with less are ubiquitous. Our shrinking computers with more and more power and functionality, to the more fuel-efficient vehicles, heaters, refrigerators, washers, and homes are just a few. The principle of "doing more with less" is fundamental to design science problem solving. It offers a way to take care of all of humanity's evolving needs with increasingly fewer resources per person. Without it, we will not be able to take care of 7 or more billion people at the standards of living that we would all desire.

One way to measure human progress is to chart our ability to do more with less. As we learn more, our understanding of systems in nature increases our ability to get more useful units of life-support for more people with less investment of resources per unit. If our technological systems are a reflection of our understanding of the principles of nature, then waste and inefficiency in our use of resources, disregard for our environment, and neglect of impoverished populations, are reflections of ignorance.

Because we do not learn less, each time resources are employed to do a given task, processes can often be designed or redesigned so that more is accomplished with the same amount of resources. For example, the first telephone wires carried two signals simultaneously. More advanced technology enabled wires to become thinner and thinner while carrying more and more signals until it became possible for wires to be eliminated altogether. A one-quarter ton communications satellite now outperforms 175,000 tons of transoceanic cable.

The Earth's resources, which now adequately support 65 to 80% of humanity,[15] need to be employed to support 100%. The only way of doing this, without draconian reductions in quality of life and choice—or drastic, genocidal, reductions of human population, is to do more with less.

6. Increasing WEALTH

Wealth is the capacity of a society to deal with present and future contingencies. It is not money, but what we do with our information, energy, and materials. One measure of wealth is the degree to which we have rearranged our environment so that it is able to support as many lives, for as long as possible, with increasing degrees of freedom, in as many conditions, at a high standard of living.

Wealth is also not measured by money, and well-being is not measured by gross national product. Wealth is knowing what to do with energy; it is know-how plus energy and materials applied to meet human needs.

Existing political and economic systems often assume the basis of wealth is the accumulation of physical resources or the ability to wield power. This assumption ignores the concept and implications of doing more with less and leads to the mistaken conclusion that there are not enough resources to go around—and so some of us are doomed to lives of brutal poverty, or worse. This false assumption of scarcity also provides a logic for war and the preemptive arming of your side so as to be prepared for an eventual Armageddon

> *"* Eliminating poverty will not happen by solving problems. It will happen by creating wealth. *"*
>
> —George Lodge

type showdown with the other side to fight over the distribution of the last pieces of the last resource pies. Assuming survival belonged to the "fittest," many political systems and their leaders see competition for scarce resources as a rationale for war.

Design science is not concerned with different ways of distributing "not enough." It is concerned with developing new ways of providing enough by doing more with less. This approach brings a new perspective to the debate between economists who advocate continued economic growth and environmentalists who recognize the limits of the biosphere and who advocate stopping growth. Neither alternative is acceptable because each means that there will always be "haves" and "have-nots" in the world or that the Earth might not be able to support life in the future—the consequences of which is that we will all be "have-nots."

Design science recognizes that real wealth is generated not by the quantity of resources that can be accumulated, but by the quality of their use. The more intelligently we employ resources, the more wealth they yield. The only thing we have identified in Universe that has no apparent limits to its growth is our knowledge. The design scientist demonstrates that wealth can continuously increase even though the total quantity of physical resources in use may not. This can occur if we continuously find ways of better and better reinvestment of our know-how to get more with less.

Human time is an important resource which can be divided into two groups: *coerced time*, which is the time an individual spends doing those tasks essential to his/her survival (eating, sleeping, getting food, etc.); and *reinvestible time*, which is the time we have free to invest in thinking, learning, and designing. The design scientist is concerned with minimizing coerced time and maximizing the total reinvestible time of humans by finding ways of meeting basic human needs, and by providing productive ways for people to use their reinvestible time. Looked at this way, the concept of reinvestible time becomes a metric for measuring wealth and the value and efficacy of a given problem solving design science strategy.

"Real wealth is indestructible and without practical limit. It can be neither created nor lost — and it leaves one system only to join another—the Law of Conservation of Energy. Real wealth is not gold. Real wealth is knowing what to do with energy."

—Buckminster Fuller

7. Everyone WINS

Design science solutions result in whole system performance improvements and "winners" in government, civil society, corporate, family, and individual areas. *Everybody wins*—solutions do not take from the rich to give to the poor (redistribution), or trickle down from the rich to the poor. They involve a fundamental redesign of society's systems so that everyone is better off.

Design science is not a win/lose problem solving, planning, or economic development strategy. Neither is it what is called a win/win strategy. Both of these imply a two-party dynamic, and there are always more than two players or stakeholders in any problem of global scale. Getting what the world wants is a win/win/win solution. Or more accurately, it is a winnth solution.

A successful strategy will have at least national,

local, corporate, environmental, economic, and global winners. And, a successful strategy will ripple through all those systems, helping resolve other problems or eliminate the causes of them—as adequate nutrition eliminates many health care problems caused by lack of food, and adequate health care increases the productivity of economic systems as workers are absent less from work due to illness, and renewable and clean supplies of energy lessens the global buildup of carbon in the atmosphere and global warming.

Another aspect of the "everybody wins" principle is that overall trends of general economic improvement ("GWP is growing at 3% per year;" "the economy is booming!" etc.) are, at best, only a first order indicator of economic health. At the macro level, they do not distinguish between 'goods' and 'bads'; for example, when there is a car accident, GWP goes up. These macro indicators need to be seen in the context of local micro economic health indicators. If social indicators of wealth go up but there are pockets of poverty where these trends do not hold, we are all impoverished—just as your heart, brain, and nervous system might be in great shape, but if there is a cancerous growth in your lungs you are not healthy at all.

8. TRANSPARENCY

Transparency in the design science process is the publicly visible display of all actors and their roles, decisions, costs, resources, expenses, impacts, assumptions, goals, and accounting. All government processes, decisions and actions, as well as business practices, industrial processes, environmental impacts, and accounting of ingredients, waste and costs must be subject to open disclosure and public access.

Transparency has a power in and of itself. In decision-making and problem solving, transparency will go further toward getting what the world wants than any number of laws.[16] For example, in the US, the little known rider in the first Superfund bill (passed to clean up toxic waste sites), called the Toxic Release Inventory, mandated that every business site in the country had to disclose the chemicals that they were using and disposing of in their manufacturing and business processes. And, critically—they had to disclose this information to everyone, including the people living down the street or down wind from their site. This enforced transparency, the public knowledge of what was happening regarding toxic chemicals, *by itself*—without the aid of additional laws outlawing or restricting these chemicals—resulted in a reduction of toxic emissions by 60% in 10 years.

When everyone knows the budget numbers it's hard to hide corruption. And because they are so important to the capacity and well-being of the world, this principle needs to be applied to governments and corporations, as well as intergovernmental, non-governmental, and religious organizations and their activities, funding, and accounting.

9. CAPACITY, **not Problems**

"We are continually faced with great opportunities which are brilliantly disguised as unsolvable problems."

—Margaret Mead

Every problem has hidden in it an opportunity so powerful that it dwarfs the problem. Design science is more about building capacity than it is about solving problems. We need to see "problems" not as something that needs to be "solved," but as a symptom of something larger—the need to enlarge the capacity of a system. Another way of looking at this is to say that we need to focus on creating wealth, not just reducing poverty. When we focus on building capacity, it becomes apparent that *wealth is in the whole, not the parts.*

"Reformations and transformations are not the same thing. Reformations are concerned with changing the means systems employ to pursue their objectives. Transformations involve changes in the objectives they pursue... there is a difference between doing things right (the intent of reformations) and doing the right thing (the intent of transformations)."

—Russell Ackoff

the entire energy system and the regional and national systems of which it is a part, and see how they could be made more efficient, resilient, reliable, safe and affordable. The emphasis is on how to build up the energy system's capacity and "health," not just its output. Demand as well as supply is a part of the system. Improvements in production and distribution efficiency, lowering of demand, decentralized or distributed production, and more efficient end users are all part of the capacity-building equation. The end result might be the same—in this case,

Example 1: If the "problem" is that someone is hungry, the conventional "solution" is to get that person some food. Through building capacity, you expand the system's ability to provide food and the hungry person's ability to obtain it.

Example 2: The problem is a shortage of electric energy in a city. The standard solution is to build another large power plant. In capacity building, however, we look at

electricity for more people in the city—but the system with more overall capacity is stronger than one with just an additional power plant.

Example 3: The problem is not enough sales. The "solution" is to knock on more doors to get more sales. A regenerative development approach would expand the capacity of the system to get more sales—go on the Internet, market to other countries, try to improve the product you are trying to sell, and examine the needs of the system you are selling in for ways to expand its capacity. Building capacity focuses efforts on the context of so-called problems; it helps us to understand challenge by understanding the system it fits into. By expanding capacity, we deal with the conditions that give rise to the problem—instead of treating symptoms.

General systems theory pioneer Ross Ashby provides another view on this in his *law of requisite variety*, which states that a system, in order to survive, must be designed to have a greater capacity for change than the processes of the environment that affect it.

10. DESIGN, **not Politics**

"You never change things by fighting the existing reality. To change something, build a new model that makes the existing model obsolete."

—R. Buckminster Fuller

If politics is the art of the possible, design science is the art of making the impossible real. That is, design sees what is needed, not what is just expedient or politically easy, and figures out how to make it happen. It starts with a vision of what is needed, not what is popular. Design science seeks to find or design an artifact that solved a problem or built the capacity of a system in such a way that the source of the problem was eliminated. Design is way around the power structure or status quo. Instead of fighting it in a bloody revolution to more "fairly" redistribute the world's wealth, a design revolution could make the poor as wealthy as the richest person through providing better-designed artifacts for living.[17]

11. REGENERATION, **not Sustainability**

One way of looking at "sustainable development" is that it is a half-vast approach to vast problems. Its purpose, to make life on this planet sustainable, is, in some circles, a noble disguise for the maintenance of the status quo. Sustainable development needs to be about creating a society that can be sustained and further developed, not about sustaining the society we have.

When the status quo includes hundreds of millions of acres of degraded to destroyed farmland and leveled rainforest, depleted to exhausted fisheries and aquifers, toxics choked streams, decreasing biodiversity, and a changing climate, *sustainability*, if it means maintaining what we have for future generations, is simply not acceptable. In short, sustainable development is like the bromide, "do no evil;" it does not set the bar high enough. We can, and need, to do better than just sustain the unacceptable—or accept the present as the best we can do.

The latest improvement on sustainability is the concept of "zero emissions." Here it is not acceptable to produce just enough waste so as to not overwhelm nature's capacity to recycle our industrial by-products. The goal is to produce our goods and services in a way that there are no wastes—so that the by-products of one industrial process become the inputs for another process. In this industrial ecology we connect the waste streams from one industrial plant to the input channels of another thereby turning waste into resources. This is another noble goal, and a huge improvement on the basic notion of sustainability—but we can do better than zero.

Beyond sustainability and zero emissions

Our local and global problems and visions for what we want need to be viewed in the context of *regenerative development*.

Development is the use of resources to improve the well-being of a society. What is called sustainable development is the use of resources to improve society's well being in a way that does not destroy or undermine the support systems needed for future development. Regenerative development is the use of resources to improve society's well being in a way that builds the capacity of the support systems needed for future development. What sustainable development is to traditional economic development, regenerative development is to sustainable development.

To take one example: "sustainable agriculture" refers to a process of producing food that does not degrade the ecosystems on which agriculture depends. It seeks to farm in ways that keep soil erosion at "replacement" levels. In this way, future generations will be able to farm the same land. This is a huge improvement over traditional, soil-erosion intensive farming, *but does not go far enough*. It is now technologically possible and economically competitive to produce food while simultaneously leaving the plot of land better off—to farm in ways that not only leave roughly the same amount of soil after harvest, but actually to increase the quantity and quality of soil after harvest; that is, to farm regeneratively. Regeneration builds capacity; sustainability, at best, maintains it.

Regeneration can work across all development sectors—not just in agriculture. Every problem confronting global society can be approached through the regeneration model. The question in sustainable development is "How can we solve this problem in such a way that we sustain or do not hurt the underlying support systems?" The question in regenerative development is "How can we solve this problem in such a way that we improve the capacity of the underlying support systems?" How can we meet our needs and develop our economy in ways that result in more rain forests, more fertile soils, restocked fisheries, clean and abundant aquifers and streams, a cleaner atmosphere, and even more biodiversity?[18] After we have met our needs for basic life support and the additional goods and services that modern society identifies with the myriad and evolving definitions of the "good life"—how do we do all that in ways that make our life supporting infrastructure stronger, more resilient and diverse, deeper and more *alive* than it was before we showed up? *That* is the challenge facing humanity in the 21st century, not how do we preserve what remains of our dwindling stocks of ecosystem infrastructure.

Regenerative development seeks to increase the efficiency and capacity of our industrial and technological metabolism while providing life-support services and products for the world's population. Like zero emissions sustainability, it seeks to close all the open loops spewing waste into the environment and direct these valuable resources to places in the industrial metabolic system where they can become valued inputs. The goal is to reduce waste and close valves that allow valuable chemistries to flow out of the industrial system into natural systems, where they become known as "pollution." But regenerative development goes further.

12. Development, not GROWTH

Design science seeks to solve problems by transforming society, not merely enlarging it. Growth is an increase in size or number. Development is an increase in competence and quality of life. The ability to satisfy human needs and desires and those of others is at the core of development.

> "If we stop thinking of the poor as victims or as a burden and start recognizing them as resilient and creative entrepreneurs and value-conscious consumers, a whole new world of opportunity will open up."
>
> —C. K. Pralahad

> "Economic growth in the Third World is an opportunity, not a threat; it is our fear of Third World success, not that success itself, that is the real danger to the world economy."
>
> —Paul Krugman

13. Needs Are MARKETS

> "A necessary accompaniment to the freedom to compete and to earn profits in so doing is the duty of citizenship."
>
> —C. Marsden, BP

The design science process seeks to harness the productive capacity of the private sector. Towards that end, design solutions are seen in the context of what contribution the market economy can make to distributing and setting in place a sustainable solution delivery process.

In a corollary to the capacity-building principle, what we see as "problems" are markets awaiting the enterprising entrepreneur who can figure out how to meet those needs. Problems are unmet needs that can often be met through creative products matched to the real needs of real people.

Meeting the basic human needs of people in emerging markets requires that the product, and its marketing and financing, be creative and well thought out. Creative, even radical marketing techniques—often in a tri-sector partnership with local NGOs and government—are as important as brilliant products.

In a world where the world's needs and problems are perceived as markets, the market economy becomes a tool for regenerative solutions. In this context, poverty is a mandate for entrepreneurial innovation and creativity, not just government intervention and paternalistic imposition of top down "solutions." Moving towards an inclusive capitalism system such as this strengthens the entire global economy. Using market forces wherever possible helps ensure that "solutions" don't arrive stillborn or disappear as soon as outside funding dries up. It is becoming increasingly clear that profitability is essential for at least economic sustainability; that profit provides the incentive needed for the kinds of effort and investment needed to make solutions successful. The need to make a profit forces solutions to be products and services that are valued by customers, and which customers will pay for. And, not incidentally, puts the customer in charge, rather than a government bureaucracy. Becoming informed, active, and involved consumers—and voting with their currency, local communities invest their valuable resources in projects that benefit their families and in which they have a stake in making sure they stay viable. The poor are transformed from victims into consumers—and when informed consumers are in charge, a market place is one of the better tools for ensuring power and control is in the hands of the community.

14. Trim Tab / TIPPING POINTS

"Look at the world around you. It may seem like an immovable, implacable place. It is not. With the slightest push—in just the right place—it can be tipped."

—Malcolm Gladwell

"Trim tab" is a word taken from the vocabulary of designers and pilots of aircraft and ships. A trim tab is a device on the trailing edge of a ship's rudder. It is, in effect, a tiny rudder on the back end of the relatively large rudder that steers the ship. It is very small but it is responsible for changing the course of the ship because it takes advantage of the dynamic principles operating on the vessel by doing the most with least effort. When the trimtab moves, it creates a low-pressure area that pulls the larger rudder to one side, in turn pulling the trailing end of the ship around and changing its course.

"Tipping point" is another metaphor similar to trim tab. Tipping points are critical points of intervention or inflection where a small change can make a large qualitative or quantitative difference in the state of a system.

Trim tab is an important concept in design science. It involves determining the set of actions that can be taken to change the course of a larger system. In design science, a trim tab is the most efficient use of force and power to accomplish a desired goal. The trim-tab metaphor is used to describe an artifact specifically designed and placed in the environment at such a time and place where its effects would be maximized thereby affecting the most advantageous change with the least resources, time, and energy invested.

15. ARTIFACTS

Artifacts, in a design science sense,[19] are physical and conceptual elements that change the properties of a system and its environment. They solve a problem and/or build the capacity of a system so that the problem is solved or no longer relevant.

A physical artifact is something like a wind generator, solar cell, computer, or building. It is something that takes up space, uses materials, and consumes energy in its manufacture and use.

A conceptual artifact is something like a law, regulation or standard that raises fuel efficiency standards for motor vehicles, guarantees health care, regulates work conditions and safety, establishes building codes, trade agreements and land ownership.

Both physical and conceptual artifacts are critical to the design science process, and to making the world work for everyone. They also work in tandem—even to the point of being seen as the two sides of the same coin. Either one by itself can be impotent or a dead-end. For example, a law that makes it a crime to go hungry or to only drive a car that gets over 100 miles per gallon, is ridiculous if there is not enough food to go around or there are no cars that get that kind of mileage. On the other hand, having an abundant food supply in a world with starvation and hunger but no organizational way of getting this food from the farm, silo, or warehouse to those in need (such as a food stamp or school lunch program, or a World Food Program that delivers food to those in need), is equally ineffective.

In the design science approach to problem solving, problems are solved through artifacts, rather than by trying to change or reform human nature. As Buckminster Fuller succinctly put it, "reform the environment, not man." Bt adding new artifacts to the world, the repertoire of responses that people have to choose from expands, thereby allowing them to change their behaviors through their own volition.

Reform the environment, not man

One rationale for the emphasis on artifacts in the design science approach to problem solving is that design science does not seek to change human nature. Rather it seeks to change the environment in which humans operate, expanding their options, not limiting their choices to what someone thinks is "good." The focus is on changing the physical environment within which humanity functions, rather that attempting to reform human behavior through laws, regulations, and/or moral imperatives. The rationale for this approach is that it is more effective, efficient, respectful of human intelligence and diversity, and leads to greater innovation, capacity growth, and longer lasting solutions. Design science is not a religion dictating what is good behavior, but a science that seeks to expand options, thereby making self- or socially destructive behaviors obsolete and onerous.

16. SCALABILITY

"Scalability" is the capacity to grow from a "one-off" prototype or proof of concept design to a mass-produced society-wide deployment of a solution.

If a solution to a problem, or a product or service for a market cannot be scaled up from the prototype stage to wide spread adoption and use, it is stillborn. A brilliant local solution that doesn't scale up is only half "complete," at best. The job of regenerative development is to move good solutions from local prototype or proof of concept to full-scale global implementation.

Scalability works both ways: the discipline of looking to scale enriches the prototype by making it more universal, robust and adaptable. Part of any good design science solution needs to be a plan for how an artifact goes from test to prototype to widespread use—or in other words, from local to regional to global impact.

17. Make Visible the INVISIBLE

"What information consumes is rather obvious: it consumes the attention of its recipients. Hence a wealth of information creates a poverty of attention, and a need to allocate that attention efficiently among the overabundance of information sources that might consume it."

—Herbert Simon

Our abilities to solve problems are dependent upon our ability to recognize and communicate problems. Because most of "reality" occurs outside the range of human senses, our ability to "make visible the invisible" is an essential part of design science.

Not only is it essential for recognizing and defining the problem, it is needed for the communication of a design science strategy and its rationale, impacts, costs, and benefits in such a way that it is understandable by all the stakeholders who will implement, benefit, pay for, or be impacted by the strategy.

Making visible the invisible, turning data into knowledge—and turning that knowledge into action— that solves problems and meets human needs, is what design science is all about. This data visualization process is often achieved by graphically decelerating events that occur too swiftly to be seen or understood, and/or by accelerating the events that occur too slowly, or are too small or big, for our perception. The following are a few methods by which the invisible can be made more visible (a more definitive list can be found in the *Methodology* section):

Modelling is a technique for taking an understanding of the state of a system and how its components interact and representing these in another medium (e.g. computer code). The model can then be manipulated to test the validity of this understanding, explore sensitivities, or calculate the consequences of these interactions over time. A commonly used simple model is '*trending*', which is plotting data about particular aspects of the system over time, allowing the design scientist to perceive patterns of change occurring too rapidly or too slowly to be evident by direct observation.

Hierarchical organizing is the process of arranging data with respect to its size, shape, form, magnitude, complexity, or other quality it might possess.

Location/distribution mapping is a technique for displaying data on maps to demonstrate the shape, size, pattern and/or location of events and their relationship to their environment. This method permits recognition of special relationships that might not be found in charts.[20]

18. The Design INITIATIVE

"Never doubt that a small group of thoughtful, committeed people can change the world. Indeed, it is the only thing that ever has."

—Margaret Mead

A design scientist does not wait to be hired or receive a mandate from the status quo to develop solutions to problems. As a source of disruptive innovations, design science seeks to do what is needed, not what there is a job to do. Design science takes initiatives that set in motion the changes needed to reach a preferred state.

Design science, somewhat unlike traditional science that seeks to understand some facet of the universe, has as its ultimate goal the taking of action that solves a basic human need problem.

The "design initiative" is the unsolicited taking on and solving of a global or local problem. Given the moral vision of design science, that it our responsibility as members of global society to solve the problems of society, one does not wait to be hired by a government, corporation, or non-profit organization to do what

is right. The design scientist sees what needs to be done and does it. The design scientist considers all of humanity the client, not just the person with the most economic wherewithal.

One of the tasks of the design scientist is to take the economic, technological, and moral initiative by designing regenerative, affordable solutions to society's problems, demonstrate their practicality and need, and place them in the environment where they can be used.

Design science brings about change through innovation—and therefore often upsets the status quo. Such disruptive innovations, or "creative trouble making" are the core of making the world's resources meet the needs of 100% of humanity.

"The young do not know enough to be prudent, and therefore they attempt the impossible—and achieve it, generation after generation."

—Pearl S. Buck

19. Moral VISION

"What is worthy and right is never impossible."

—Henry Ford

At the core of design science is a set of values that say that it is unacceptable for some of the people of the world to die of starvation and all other "curable" causes and the rest of us are be sentenced to watch this horror via our numerous communications links. This moral vision dictates that what is "right" from a perspective of enhancing the quality and length of life for all takes precedence over what is important monetarily for the few. Meeting the basic human needs of the world trumps the accumulation of ever-larger quantities of money and shareholder value for its own sake.[21]

The moral vision of design science is based on the assumption that each individual is better off when every individual is better off, and that it is the responsibility of those who understand this principle to act on it. The *design initiative* described above is based on this assumption.

The moral vision of design science, plus its practical, pragmatic problem solving methodology, seeks to make the impossible possible, practical, and profitable.

"In a country well governed, poverty is something to be ashamed of. In a country badly governed, wealth is something to be ashamed of."

—Confucius

The next part of the primer, the methodology section, is intended to help you take the design initiative. It is a step-by-step guide to the design science process.

BIBLIOGRAPHY

PLANNING

Russell Ackoff, *Redesigning the Future*

Russell Ackoff, Redesigning Society

Russell Ackoff, *Beating the System: Using Creativity to Outsmart Bureaucracies*

Russell Ackoff, *Idealized Design*

Stafford Beer, *Platform fro Change*

Graham Friend, Stefan Zehle, *Guide To Business Planning*

Erich Jantsch, *Perspectives of Planning*

Rolf Smith, *The Seven Levels of Change*

UNITAR, *Planning in Developing Countries, Theory and Methodology*

United Nations, *Long-Term Planning*

Anthony J. Dolman, editor, *Global Planning and Resource Management*

Ian McHarg, *Design With Nature*

Ian McHarg, *Towards a Comprehensive Plan for Environmental Quality*

WORLD

Buckminster Fuller, *Operating Manual for Spaceship Earth*

Buckminster Fuller, *Nine Chains to the Moon*

Buckminster Fuller, *Utopia or Oblivion*

Buckminster Fuller, *Earth Inc.*

Nicholas Georgiescu-Roegen, *The Entropy Law and the Economic Process*

Howard Odum, *Energy, Power and Society*

Jared Diamond, *Guns, Germs and Steel*

Jeffrey A. Rosensweig, *Winning the Global Game*

Kevin Kelly, *Out of Control*

Michael Rothschild, *Bionomics*

Paul Hawken, Amory Lovin, Huntr Lovins, *Natural Capitalism,*

Thomas L. Friedman, *The World is Flat*

Thomas L. Friedman, *The Lexus and the Olive Tree*

John Brockman, *The Next Fifty Years*

William Knoke, *Bold New World*

Manuel Castells, *The Rise of the Network Society*

Medard Gabel, Henry Bruner, *Global Inc.: An Atlas of the Multinational Corporation*

Medard Gabel, *Energy, Earth, and Everyone*

Medard Gabel, *Ho-Ping: Food for Everyone*

World Resources Institute, *World Resources (bi-annual)*

Worldwatch Institute, *Vital Signs*

World Bank, *World Development Report*, (annual)

United Nations Development Programme, *Human Development Report*

Science Magazine (weekly)

The Economist (weekly)

POVERTY

Jeffrey Sachs, *The End of Poverty*

J. F. Rischard, *High Noon*

Stephen Smith, *Ending Global Poverty*

Robert Chambers, *Ideas For Development*

BUSINESS AND DEVELOPMENT

C. K. Prahalad, *The Fortune at the Bottom of the Pyramid*

Stuart Hart, *Capitalism at the Crossroads*

Melissa Everett, *Making a Living While Making a Difference*

John Elkington, Pamela Hartigan, *The Power of Unreasonable People*

Marc J. Epstein, *Making Sustainability Work*

STATE OF THE UNIVERSE

Tao The King, by Lao Tzu (Archie J. Bahm translation)

The Bhagavad-Gita

The Upanishads

Yoga Philosophy of Patanjali

Black Elk Speaks, by John G. Neihardt

Synergetics, Vol. 1 and 2 by Buckminster Fuller

Out of My Later Years, or *Ideas and Opinions* by Albert Einstein

Systems Thinking, edited by F. E. Emery

Living Systems, by James G. Miller

The Structure of Scientific Revolutions, by Thomas S. Kuhn

The Character of Physical Law, by Richard Feynman

The Nature of the Physical World, by Arthur Eddington

What is Life? and *Mind and Matter*, by Erwin Schrodinger

Equations of Eternity, by David Darling

The Life of the Cosmos, by Lee Smolin

Design for Evolution, by Erich Jantsch

Nonzero: The Logic of Human Destiny, by Robert Wright

The Age of Spiritual Machines, by Ray Kurzwell

The Lives of a Cell, by Lewis Thomas

The Hidden Connections, by Fritjof Capra

The World Treasury of Physics, Astronomy and Mathematics, edited by Timothy Ferris

The View From the Center of the Universe, by Joel R. Primack and Nancy Abrams

ENDNOTES

1 Design Council, *Annual Review 2002*, London, Design Council, 2002, p. 19.

2 The descriptions of present planning methods and design science are derived from Russell Ackoff. *Design for the Future*, etc.

3 All systems are part of a hierarchy of systems; it is critical to design science to maintain the same level of aggregation in analysis, synthesis and design of solutions. This means, for example, that if you are looking at global energy systems, that you don't analyze the world's oil reserves, hydro capacity, wind potential, and the fuel efficiency of a single car. In this case, the level of aggregation is the world, and a single car and world are an obvious mismatch.

4 Other explanations, implications, and design suggestions of this rule say that those components of a system that have the greatest flexibility and freedom are the most powerful. More technically, it says that the greater the variety within a system, the greater its ability to reduce variety in its environment through regulation; in active regulation only variety can destroy variety. The variety of perturbations a system can potentially be confronted with is nearly unlimited, so trying to maximize the internal variety (or diversity) of a design, so as to be optimally prepared for any foreseeable or unforeseeable contingency is a good idea. Yet another spin-off of this rule is that a system can only model or control something to the extent that it has sufficient internal variety to represent it.

5 *Earth's Speed* http://members.aol.com/nlpjp/speed.htm

6 "Death Throes of a Crippler," *New York Times*, May 27, 2003

7 WHO, *Removing Obstacles to Healthy Development* (Geneva, WHO, 1999, p. 29).

8 Jeffrey Sachs, "Doing the sums on Africa," (*The Economist*, May 22, 2004, p.19).

9 Ibid.

10 E. K. Pilitch, et. al. "Ecosystem-based Fishery Management," (*Science*, July 16, 2004, p. 346).

11 Buckminster Fuller, *Utopia or Oblivion*, (New York. Bantam Books, 1968)

12 Paul Hawken, Amory Lovins, Hunter Lovins, *Natural Capitalism*, (New York, Little, Brown, 1999, p.14). 6% of the vast flows of materials in the U.S. economy end up as products.

13 E. von Weizsacker et al.; *Factor Four: Doubling Wealth, Halving Resource Use* (Earthscan, London, 1996).

14 Paul Hawken, Amory Lovins, Hunter Lovins, *Natural Capitalism*, (New York, Little, Brown, 1999. p. 12).

15 This percentage depends on how one defines "adequately supported." The book *The Bottom Billion* by Paul Collier points out that, in 2007, there were 6.5 billion people in the world, and that the least wealthy billion, the "bottom billion" are the ones who are not adequately supported by the world's resources and wealth.

16 Ann Florini, "The End of Secrecy." Foreign Policy, Summer, 1998. P.50.

17 M. Gabel. "Buckminster Fuller and the Game of the World" in *Buckminster Fuller: Anthology for the New Millennium* (New York. St, Martin's Press, 2001). For a more through explication of Fuller's design methodology see: B. Fuller, "Universal Requirements for a Dwelling Advantage" in *No More Second Hand God* (Southern Illinois University Press, 1962) and B. Fuller, "Design Science Event Flow" in *Utopia or Oblivion* New York. Bantam Books, 1968)

18 Bioengineering, genetic engineering are here to stay. Focusing them on restoring lost species, rather than cloning new "Frankensteins" is a more regenerative path for this science. Incentives need to be established for this use of genetic engineering.

19 The term "artifact" in a scientific sense often refers to something that gets into a science experiment and produces bogus results. In imaging, whether photographic, medical, or scientific, "artifact" refers to limitations of the imaging technology that results in misrepresentations of the object being imaged that are a result of the technology being used, and not reflective of the characteristic of the object being imaged. The two meanings are entirely different and unrelated, other than by spelling.

20 If one is mapping issues on a global scale it is important that the base map is accurate. An inaccurate map of the world will lead to inaccurate data representation, and distorted or non-existent relationships and patterns. One tool for global resource and issue mapping is the Fuller projection map. It is the least distorted two-dimensional map of the whole Earth. See http://www.bfi.org for more information

21 It should be noted that this is not a screed against capitalism or the market economy. Design science sees both as powerful tools for creating and distributing wealth. It is rather a setting of moral priorities.

PART 2

METHODOLOGY

Recipes for Revolution

Design Science Planning Process

Our job: Design a set of actions that get us from the Problem/Present State to the Preferred State.

Problem/ Present State	ACTIONS	Preferred State

Design and Plan for Implementation:
- Who does what, when, where, and how
- What human, natural resources and technology are needed?
- What is the cost and were do we get the funding?

What criteria will we use to evaluate our options?

How will we measure success?

More specifically:

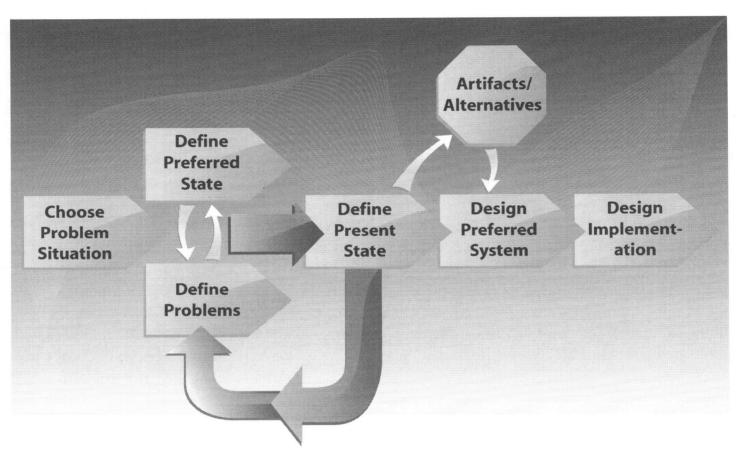

"A revolution is not a dinner party, or writing an essay, or doing embroidery;
it cannot be so refined, so leisurely and gentle, so temperate, kind, courteous,
restrained and magnanimous."

—Mao Zedong, 1927

The flow-diagrams on the first two pages of this section outline the design science process. It takes the design scientist from problem recognition through a systematic and comprehensive design process in which the goal or target (the Preferred State) that the designer is aiming for is clarified, make explicit and used as the guiding force in developing the overall strategic design and plan that gets us to the Preferred State.

PART 2: METHODOLOGY

> **Methodology:** 1. The system of principles, procedures, and practices applied to a particular branch of knowledge; 2. a manner or means of procedure, especially a systematic and regular way of accomplishing a given task

THE DESIGN SCIENCE PLANNING PROCESS

The design science planning process is a method by which individuals or small groups can solve complex real-world problems. It facilitates the development of alternative solutions to problems, and strategic designs and plans for implementing those solutions. It identifies what needs to be done, when it needs to be done, by who, and in what sequence, as well as identify what resources are needed to implement the design. And, it does this within the conceptual framework presented in the preceding section of this book.

> Design is not a book, or a set of procedures. It is, at its core, a creative *act*. It is this action— what you do to attain a desired goal, that this document is all about. Given that, this section of the *Design Science Primer* includes activities for your or your team to do. These will be highlighted in boxes like this one.

> What should we focus on and where in that great buzzing confusion of the world will it be most efficient for us to apply our energy, intellect, time and passion so that we have the most impact?

1. Start Up:
RECOGNIZING the Problem Situation/CHOOSING the Problem

"It isn't that they can't see the solution. It is that they can't see the problem."
—C. K. Chesterton

"The only way of understanding a system is to understand the system it fits into."
—Howard Odum

Where do *you* start? Where do *we* start?

We start with our values.

> **To do:** What are the world's three most important problems? What is the world's *most* important problem? What is the problem you feel most perturbed about? What situation or problem in the world, if you think about it, gets you angry? What geographical area of the world are you most concerned about? How is the problem you want to deal with related to everything else? Draw a diagram of how it is related. What would you do with $5 million to deal with the problem you feel most strongly about?

We start with what we see, or what we *feel*, as the problem we want to solve. *And then we back up.*

What is the area your problem fits into? Maybe you think that the lack of food—hunger— in the poorer regions of the world is an outrage, and that this is the problem with which you want to deal. What does hunger in a specific region of the world fit into? What is the larger system of which it is a part?

It is important to realize that what we normally see as a "problem" is really the symptoms of a deeper problem. When we back up to the larger system(s) the underlying problem begins to become visible. We need to ask, *what causes the symptoms that we think of as the problem?*

One way of looking at the hunger problem in, for example the South Sudan, is to see it in the context of larger and interlocking geographical, geopolitical, cultural, ideological, and ecological systems. Whether it is the bioregion, a village or nation, every problem we address is part of larger systems.

We always start with the larger system. (And remember, until you get to the Universe, there is always a larger system.) If we defined our problem as the lack of food in a village in South Sudan, we might find ourselves limited to the options available in the local food system. We would likely see a "solution" as way of expanding the local food supply from local resources. And if this were to happen, we would miss over 95% of the available possible solutions to the problem. *Thinking "outside the box" is thinking outside the system the problem is within.*

Expanding the scope of the problem, so it is not just a village or even the country that the village is located within, enlarges the number of options and the way

---

1. Choose the Problem.

we look at the problem. In the South Sudan village example, enlarging the problem from a lack of food in a poor African country to the global food, ecological, economic and technological systems will allow us to see options that were not present in the smaller system. From this perspective, solving the problem often becomes a question of what can we introduce from outside the local problem system that will bring about the changes we are seeking.

The first step of the design science planning process is deciding what problem(s) or direction(s) you or your group will pursue. This is not easy, and it is critical to the eventual success of our work. The values, perspective, interests, resources, and talents of the designer(s) undertaking this initiative will help determine the design project. Determining and clarifying these values is essential. Answering the questions in the cube will help in this process.

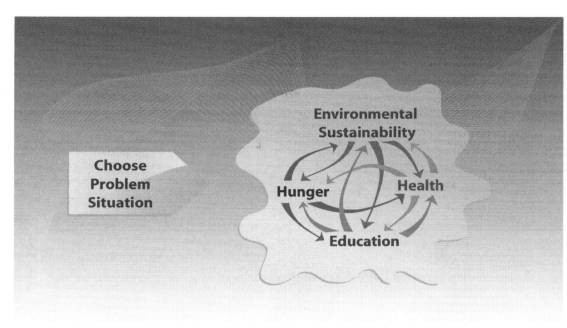

Choose Mess ⇒ Choose/recognize problem situation ⇒

Mess vs. Problem

> Start with the mess. Look for the big picture.

We don't start out with problems all neatly prearranged for us to solve. The real world is not arranged like a fath textbook. Usually, a problem situation or "mess"

confronts us. *Good problem solving does not start off with assuming we know what the problem is.*

If you accept given prepackaged problems, you will be starting out with hidden, predetermined assumptions that can interfere with developing a creative response to the real problems causing the situation we are seeking to fix.

The difference between a mess and a problem is that a mess is something you are aware of in the environment and a problem is something you construct rationally to assist in understanding and effecting change in the environment. *Messes are given; problems you define and construct.* Problems are your perceptions of why and how a mess is a mess. Once you define what the "problem" is, you have bought into a lot of self-limiting and hidden assumptions that curtail the options you have. We need to take care to define the problem, not its symptoms, from a context and perspective that will provide us with the options needed to reach the Preferred State.

Seeing "problems" is the problem. If we choose a problem without looking at its context, we limit our thinking and perceptions of possible alternatives. One way to de-problemize the design process is to take the "problem" and ask and define *what is the Preferred State* for the situation that the problem is embedded within? What should the situation look like, how should the system perform? This exercise will move us away from the particulars of the "problem"— the symptoms of systemic dysfunction, to the behaviors of the whole system we are seeking to change to what we have defined an the Preferred State.

The chart on the previous page describes the start of the design science process. A general "problem situation"—not a specific problem— is chosen. The context for a specific problem is the problem situation. Every problem has a larger system of which it is a part. The "problem situation" is what your values tell you are important (hungry people, illiteracy, lack of access to health care, environmental destruction, etc.). From this general area of concern you both zoom-in to a specific problem you want to address, and zoom-back to take a big picture view of the problem area. For example, you zoom-in to identify malnutrition in rural villages, and you zoom-out to the global food, economic, technological and ecological systems.

There are many approaches a design science planning team can take in choosing a problem situation. The following are three that have been used by groups at previous design science planning sessions.

1. Focus on a specific functional area of human life-support, such as food or shelter, and develop a strategy for meeting these needs at a chosen geographical scale (from global to individual dwelling) or at a trans-boundary level.

2. Choose a particular geographical area, such as a neighborhood, region, or nation, and develop a strategy for that defined region which includes one or more of the functional life-support areas.

3. Take one of the trans-boundary categories (such as urban areas or slums), and develop a solution to a basic human need in that category for a specific part of the world.

Examples of areas of human needs:
Food
Water
Shelter
Sanitation
Health Care
Education
Energy
Transportation
Communications
Materials
Recreation
Logistics
Environment

Examples of geographic scales for focus:
Individual
Dwelling unit
Neighborhood/Community
City
State region
State
National region
Nation
Global region
Global

Examples of Trans- boundary levels of focus:
Climatic region /bio-region/water shed
Economic status

Geographical and Economic status (urban slums, rural poverty)
Level of technology use
Religion or other cultural dynamic
Market access

If you choose to work with an area of human needs, you need to define the geographic scale on which you want to focus. If you are planning the development of a specific geographic region, then you need to decide which functional areas, at that level, on which you want to work.

It is important to remember that, at whatever level your focus, design science problem solving should move from the general to the specific—from the "whole" to the parts—from the generalized principle to the special case. In design science, problem recognition starts at the global level and works down to the local level, thus insuring that all subsequent strategies or artifacts developed locally are compatible with global potentials and restraints.

Functional Definitions

The next step is to develop working definitions of the functional area or areas with which you will be dealing. A *functional definition* describes the designed operation or role that the system under consideration plays in the larger system. For example, each part of humanity's external metabolic system (see Part 1, page __), plays an essential role in the operation of that system just as each part of our internal metabolic system plays an essential role in the operations of our bodies. This role is a specific function that needs to be performed in order for the rest of the system to work properly—to maintain itself and to continue to thrive and evolve. The functional definition describes the particular function the area being studied plays in the larger system. It describes what the system *does*.

For example, if we are focusing on energy supply for Africa:

What is the definition of energy?
"The capacity to do work."
What role does it perform in the system for which you are seeking to develop a solution?

In supplying energy to rural areas of Africa, energy is used to power food production, water pumping, vehicles, lighting and economic activities.

2. Envisioning the PREFERRED STATE

---

2. Define the goal.

The chart below describes the next step of the design science process. Having chosen a general problem situation and a more specific problem within that area, we now determine its *Preferred State*. We do this by listing the qualities of a state that is preferable to the problem situation.

Envisioning the Preferred State

"Don't insult the future. Anything is possible."

—French proverb

Start with the Whole

Design science strategic planning, problem solving and capacity building begins with the definition of success— not the failure of the system being looked at. Starting with the "problem" is beginning with the failure of the system. Beginning with the "Preferred State"— what the system should be doing if it were healthy and functioning the way we want it to, is starting with the goal and direction. It is a more powerful problem solving method, as it does not exclude as many options from potential strategic designs and plans.

A Preferred State is, among other things, performance standards for a healthy system, and as such it is the direction we want to be going. Defining the Preferred State is stating our goals. It is the translation of our values and vision into a description of an ideal situation.

As a set of objectives, the Preferred State is our vision of the desired functioning of the system for which we are going to plan. It is our definition of success and forms the foundation of the decision-making criteria that we use to evaluate options and designs.

A Preferred State is the design of the system according to our values, vision and perspective. Political and economic constraints are removed. Technology and operational viability are the two constraints governing the design of the Preferred State—which needs to use present day technology and known resources. The Preferred State describes what we want, not what we think is probable or will be permitted. It is not a prediction of what we think will or can happen. Rather, it is a bold statement of what we want to happen. It is

Define Preferred State

Choose Problem Situation

Define Problems

often revolutionary and transformative, not evolutionary or incremental. The Preferred State is in stark contrast to what politicians and bureaucrats think is practicable, expedient, or currently affordable.

Part of the conceptual environment of the Preferred State is knowing what the "business as usual" or extrapolative future will be. This is the linear extension of current trends into the future. In this future, the future looks like today, only bigger. In many cases, extrapolating present trends into the future breaks the system. For example, projecting present carbon-intensive energy use and growth into the future overwhelms the environment's ability to absorb the waste products of such growth.

Another way of looking at the Preferred State is that it is an aspirational future. It is what we want or aspire to, not what we are afraid of. It is not a "needs assessments" but goal clarification. As such, it is a powerful tool for bringing about and managing change.

There are many tools for trying to guess or predict the future, but the key tools for creating the future are aspirations and the development of a technologically possible Preferred State. With a clearly defined Preferred State comes a shared vision, core values, appropriate options, and a set of decision making criteria that guides the entire design science process.

Part of the process of developing the Preferred State is to suspend all constraints except for those of technological feasibility and ecological integrity. We answer the question, "What would an ideal future look like? What would it do? and, "How would it work?"

Defining the Preferred State forces you to make explicit what you want and where you want to go. This step involves developing a working hypothesis which you will test and document as you develop a complete strategy. For example, if your Preferred State includes providing adequate nutrition for every human on Earth, the plan you develop then becomes an experiment to test if the goal is possible and how it might be brought about.

Defining a Preferred State can be a simple brainstorming game. Extensive research and technical analysis are unnecessary for determining what you *want*. As Russell Ackoff points out, "there are no experts for what should be." Everyone has an equal right to contribute and help form the goals in the planning process.

Frames of Reference

Another way of viewing the Preferred State is to see it as a frame of reference to the present situation. This provides a perspective from which to view the difference between what is happening and what should be happening. A physician diagnoses a patient based on knowledge of a "healthy" or Preferred State functioning of the body. Problems can be better understood by referencing them against as clear as possible a notion of how the system should be working. Though humans rarely define a Preferred State for society and use this as a tool for understanding and resolving our problems, it is essential in order to plan for the future.

A design team often develops a Preferred State by first generating a set of general values shared by the group and then comparing them to a set of values that are known to be operative in the problem state. From these preferred values you can develop an outline of those preferred characteristics of the system you are planning. For example, if you value conservation of material resources as opposed to excessive waste of resources, the description of your Preferred State would reflect that value: e.g. packaging should be designed in such a way that it can either be reused or readily recycled.

The following is an example of a Preferred State

47

> "The future is not to be predicted,
> it is to be planned."
> —John Platt

developed by a design science group that focused on the global food situation:

- Given the present global food problems, a Preferred State would be one in which sufficient nutritionally sound food for all of humanity's healthful survival and evolution is available on a regenerative, non-depleting basis.
- A global food system should allow for maximum individual flexibility in food types to permit as much cultural diversity as possible.
- Food should be a birthright, not an economic weapon of exploitation.
- The food system, as well as the food, should be safe. For example, farm workers as well as food should not be exposed to dangerous pesticides.
- There should be as little coerced human labor involved in the food system as possible.
- The global food system should be regenerative; that is, it should not be based on resources which are rapidly being depleted such as fossil fuels and it should not be based on short-sighted practices such as poor soil management.
- The food system should have the least possible negative environmental impacts and the most possible possitive impact as possible, such as the build-up of poor soils into rich soils.
- There should be an optimum diversity of food crops and a diversity of different strains within each crop. There should be an overall genetic bank increase.
- There should be a minimal dependence on adverse fluctuations in natural cycles.

- The global food system should operate at maximum efficiency—in terms of energy, materials, land and human time use in all stages of the food system.
- There should be a built-in flexibility in the system; there should be a back-up storage system to insure the maximum amount of nutritionally sound food to maximize the number of forward days for all of humanity.
- The fear of an inadequate food supply should be vanquished. Planning and management of the global system should be as comprehensive and anticipatory as possible to insure a guaranteed rgenerative supply of food for everyone.
- A global food system should have a high amount of monitoring and feedback for quality and quantity control.
- Access to all accurate food information should be as high as possible.
- There should be a maximum amount of research and development related to improving the food system.

The groupings of characteristics used in the Preferred State can be used to describe general categories of preferred characteristics, such as:

DISTRIBUTION

This describes the preferred *availability* of a life-support service that the system under consideration is intended to produce. Since providing adequate life-support for all humanity is the general goal of design science, considering the distribution of a service or product is critical.

PERFORMANCE

This describes the preferred system in terms of its capacity to produce life-support goods and services with the minimum possible investment of resources and the minimum amounts of waste produced in the process.

ENVIRONMENTAL IMPACTS

This describes the environmental impacts of the Preferred State. To minimize negative or disruptive effects on the environment, this step must be carefully described. Designing with nature is fundamental to design science because it is the only way we can assure our long-term sustainable health and well being.

MAINTENANCE AND CHANGE

This describes how the system is to be managed and regulated and how future changes in the design can be implemented. This is very important in relation to the popular acceptance and long-term survivability of the system.

Our descriptions of a Preferred State will change and evolve as we explore new ways of seeing problems and developing options for reaching the Preferred State.

As our personal values, vision or perspective change, our Preferred State descriptions will change. It is very useful to repeat this Preferred State formulation step over again (and again) in order to clarify the common objectives of the planning team. Such an exercise

> "Where you are headed is more important than how fast you are going. Rather than always focusing on what's urgent, learn to focus on what is really important."
>
> —Stephen Covey

> "The only way of discovering the limits of the possible is to venture a little way past them into the impossible."
>
> —Arthur C. Clarke

functions as a reality check on the design science process.

A helpful exercise in developing a long-range strategy is to describe the preferred system and to work backward to the present describing the necessary steps that lead to your goal. As you work backward to the present, you will find it is helpful to frame the different steps in the prevailing social context so that the plan appears both logical and implementable. For example, you could identify actual institutions, organizations, agencies and individuals either engaging in or capable of engaging in the prescribed steps of the strategy.

Problem State v.1.0

Simultaneously with the development of the Preferred State, we create a first draft of the problem state. In this case, the problem state is the inverse of the Preferred State. For example, if the Preferred State is "the provision of abundant supplies of clean and affordable energy to all," some of the components of a problem state embedded within this Preferred State are:

- Inadequate supplies of energy
- Current supplies of energy are not clean
- Current supplies of energy are not affordable to many

3. DEFINING the Problem State

"The formulation of the problem is often more essential than its solution"

—Albert Einstein

After the Preferred State and the Problem State have been defined for the first time, the Present State is described.

> 3. Define the problem, not the solution.

DESCRIBING THE PROBLEM STATE *is the step in the planning process where we define what is wrong.* The Problem State description should reflect the inadequacies of the present situation.

Recognizing and defining problems is a difficult and critical task. We are familiar with news reports and analyses of current events in the media. Usually what we call problems are really only symptoms of problems. Symptoms are the visible effects of a problem, while the problems themselves are usually related to the functional or structural characteristics of a system. Distinguishing between symptoms and problems is important in making more accurate definitions of the problems we want to resolve — and in developing solutions that actually bring about the changes we want. Treating symptoms doesn't solve problems. At best, it makes us feel like we are doing something, but often the result is another, equally or more serious problem.

The way we describe the problem depends on the lenses you use to see and the yardsticks you use to measure. The Problem State is what is not working in the system we want to change. Collaborative problem solving and strategic design and planning brings multiple perspectives to the recognition and definition of a problem. As more people come to grips with the complexity of a problem, the richness of its description increases. And, as this happens, more alternatives emerge that will get us to the Preferred State.

Everyone brings his or her own frames of

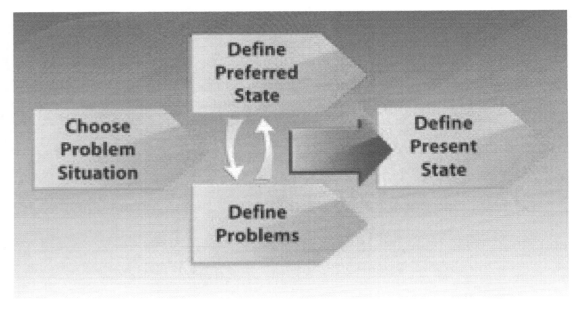

reference to the design science planning process. These perspectives are based on different political, economic, cultural, psychological, organizational, and religious values and experiences. It is important to understand when and how we use these perspectives and to see the degree to which our own cultural frame of values affects the way we define problems. However useful these frames of reference may be in organizing our ideas of the problem, we must take care to see that they do not inhibit, limit, or predetermine our understanding of the descriptions that we will develop in the course of stating the problem.

As indicated on the design science planning process diagram at the beginning of this section, we should repeat the Problem State description step several times until we are satisfied with our statement of the problems. In the first run through of the Problem State step, we will usually generate a list of preliminary questions and statements of the problem. After we have worked through the next steps, we can return to the Problem State step and refine our problem state descriptions. During this refinement, we will often find that different aspects of the problem can be grouped under certain functional categories.

Refined descriptions of the Problem State will usually include the following four groups of characteristics:

DISTRIBUTION

This refers to availability or access to something that meets a need, and whose absence creates a problem. A problem can be described in terms of distribution if everyone is not receiving or does not have access to a particular life-support system. For example, if 50% of a given population does not have adequate daily food nutrition in spite of sufficient known food supplies in the given region, then the distribution in the Problem State is important.

PERFORMANCE

This refers to the efficiency of something that meets a need or to the production of that need-meeting item. These characteristics are usually described in terms of the system's capacity to produce life-support goods and services with the minimum possible investment of resources and the minimum possible amounts of wastes produced in the process. For example, the U.S. transportation system depends almost entirely on petroleum. A problem statement of this system could describe the performance of each of the different modes in terms of passenger or freight miles per invested resources and the efficiency of each process.

ENVIRONMENTAL IMPACTS

This refers to the negative, disruptive effects the present system has on the environment. These are often stated in terms of pollution levels, breakdowns in ecological cycles, environmental diseases, and depletion or damage to environmental resources and services, including the degradation of species, land, soil quality, minerals, air, and water.

MAINTENANCE AND CHANGE

This refers to aspects of the system that regulate and change the system. These characteristics aften appear when antiquated or misguided government or other regulation and inflexibility in a system's functioning limit its ability or effectiveness in providing essential life-support services. If the system cannot be changed by its users to better provide for needs, then this characteristic should be described as part of the Problem State. For example, if a region depends entirely on natural gas for heating, or all its food comes from long distances, and there are no mechanisms for people to convert their heating systems to other forms of heating or conservation, or there are no ways obtaining food from local suppliers, then the system is so rigid that there is a problem.

The following is an example of the energy Problem State described in a Global Solutions Lab energy strategy:

Global Energy Problem State

- *Not enough* energy available for 100% of humanity's life-support, e.g., 1 billion people without access to electricity; there are "blackouts," "brownouts" and fuel rationing; there is little or no industrial energy available to construct and further develop life-support systems.
- *Inequitable distribution* of energy; for example, the United States, with 5% of the world's population, consumes over 20% of the world's energy.
- *Low efficiency* of energy conversion, such as appliances that waste electricity, cars that get low mileage per gallon of fuel, materials that require a lot of energy used in place of low-energy-costing materials, uninsulated structures, etc. Present-day energy converters average 4–5% over-all thermal and mechanical efficiency. For every 100 barrels of oil produced, approximately 95, as far as doing productive work, go down the drain. An overall efficiency of at least 12-20% is feasible with present-day design and engineering know-how.
- *Negative environmental impact* of energy use in the global energy system; e.g. resource depletion, waste, pollution of air, water and land by unwanted chemicals, heat and noise; and disruption of ecological cycles through strip mining, waste and pollution; in short, an environment whose capacity to provide what we are demanding of it, and to absorb what we are injecting into it, is rapidly being overwhelmed.
- *Over-dependence* on limited energy resources, such as fossil and nuclear fuels.

"There is no such thing as a social, political or economic problem. There are just problems with social, economic and technological components."

—Russell Ackoff

- *Low diversity and redundancy* of energy sources and systems; e.g., most of our "eggs" are in one basket— oil.
- *Unsafe* use of human physical labor (coal mining, oil refining, etc.).
- *Centralized* and one-way energy systems; i.e. energy flows from monopolistic utilities and corporations to individual consumers, without the inverse option.

What are the problems?

How do you define what is not working?

Group Methods for Defining the Problem

BRAINSTORMING is a group method for generating ideas. Use this technique to help define the Problem State. This helps to produce many views of the problem.

Start this activity by determining a period of time the activity will last. 10 to 15 minutes is usually sufficient. Next, define the subject or general area or system of the problem. Then ask the group to offer different ideas or views of the problems within the system. Have a member of the group list the ideas on a whiteboard or flipchart as they are suggested without modifications or arranging. The important role of brainstorming is that it allows a diverse and wide-ranging set of responses to be generated without judgment. Brainstorming is not analytic and imposes no constraints on the listing of possible ideas.

GROUP PRIORITY SETTING is a method of reducing the many views generated by a group by building consensus. Start this exercise by asking the participants to list what they think are the most important characteristics of the Problem State. Next, compile these lists to make a master list of all of the responses. After this, the group can discuss the appropriateness and priority of each statement. Then, as a group, decide on the most important statements.

SIMULATION GAMING is another method that can be used to gain an understanding of a situation. In this method the group imagines that they are in a new role and faced with a particular situation that stresses the system being examined. How will we respond?

One example of this method, used in the Global Solutions Lab, is the *Spaceship Captain Game*. This simulation has the group imagine that they are the captains of a spaceship that is in trouble. They do not know what is wrong, where their spacecraft is, or where it is going. The participants are asked, "*What do you need to know in order to identify the problems and insure the ship's survival?*"

The responses, in the form of questions, are listed on a flip chart or white board. This exercise is very useful when learning to recognize and define problems. It helps to determine what kinds of information are necessary for general problem solving.

The following are sample responses generated by this exercise:
　　How do we know there is a problem?

What are the problems?
How critical are they?
Where do we find them?
How many people do they affect and to what degree?
What resources are available to solve the problems?
Have these problems happened before?
How successful were past solutions?
What are the alternative solutions?
How would we evaluate the proposed solution?
How much time do we have to solve the problem?
What happens if we do nothing?
Where are we?
Where are we going?
Where do we want to be going?

QUESTIONS/EXERCISES

1. What is a problem?

2. What is the difference between a symptom and a problem?

3. What is a frame of reference?

4. What are your frames of reference?

5. Ask the people in your group to define the world food problem.

6. What are their hidden frames of reference?

4. DESCRIBE **the Present State**

*"Not everything that can be counted counts, and
not everything that counts can be counted."*

—Albert Einstein

> How can you describe the present state?
>
> How is the present system operating?
>
> What do you need to know?

We have to learn the present so we can invent the future. As the chart at right helps clarify, the Present State is the context for the Problem State. The Present State is the environment in which the problem is defined and out of which the preferred system will be designed.

It is critical to the design science process that the designer views all problem-solving in a reiterative manner. The first draft of the Problem State is just the first draft. As the Problem State is defined and explicated, the Preferred State gains greater clarity. Items not thought of in the initial definition of the Preferred State emerge as the Problem and Present State come into sharper focus.

In similar manner, as the chart on the right illustrates, the Preferred State functions as the context for the Present State. It is the Preferred State that provides directionality to the problem solving process and the definitions of the Problem and the Present states.

In describing the Present State, you attempt to gain a comprehensive picture—a many-faceted analysis of the present situation. The purpose of this step is to clarify critical factors of the problem that will permit you to organize data about the system under consideration and develop the most effective solutions.

Every present state requires a slightly different set of descriptive tools. Sometimes it is necessary to invent new ways of describing aspects of the system in order to understand adequately what is going on.

The following set of tools have been used to gather, organize, and make visible the information needed to make the most informed decisions about the system being considered and the possible options for a problem's resolution:

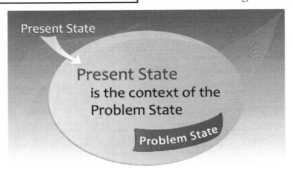

Present State ≠ Problem State

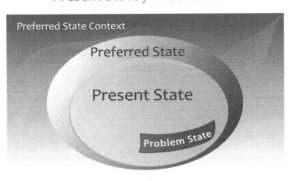

The Problem State and the alternatives to the Problem Situation are contained with the Present State.

INPUT/OUTPUT ANALYSIS is a chart or diagram that shows the inputs and outputs of a system. The "system" itself is simplified to a "black box" that has no parts. We can make an input/output diagram by outlining a system and listing what goes in and what comes out.

Simple Input/Output Chart Examples

Example 1:

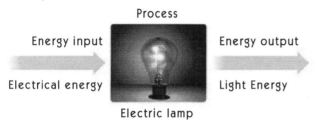

Example 2:

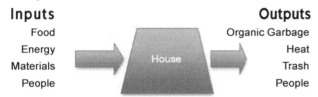

COMPONENTS/ PROCESSES/HIERARCHY are diagrams that show how the different parts and processes of a system are related. Here, that "black box" from the Input/Output chart is divided into its component parts or systems.

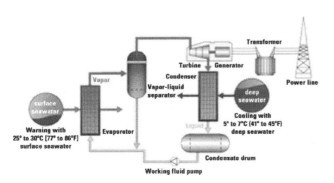

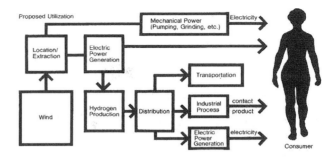

For example, your body is made up of different organs which function in different processes: your lungs are part of the respiratory system; the stomach is part of the digestive system; the heart is part of the circulatory system, etc.

You can make a components and processes diagram by graphically representing the system and indicating the components and processes involved.

RESOURCES USED/NEEDED/AVAILABLE describes what material and other resources are needed to make and maintain the system being considered.

WHO DOES WHAT/ORGANIZATIONS/ ACTORS describes or lists the organizations or groups that work in or govern the system being considered.

KEY INDICATORS are measurements that indicate the state of the system being considered. For

GLOBAL ERADICATION (% LIVING IN ABSOLUTE PROVERTY)

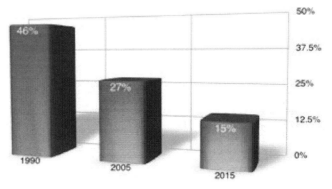

Global Surface Temperature

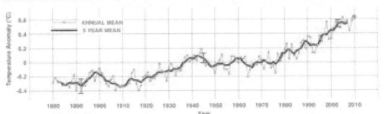

GLOBAL LAND-OCEAN TEMPERATURE INDEX

example, temperature and blood pressure are among the key indicators of an individual's health. Passenger miles, available edible protein, energy consumption, population growth rate, unemployment rates, inflation rates, efficiency ratings of tools are all examples of key indicators of different social and technological systems. You can invent new key indicators by measuring characteristics of a system that you think provide an indication of its relative health, performance, longevity, or efficiency.

TRENDS OF KEY INDICATORS are charts or

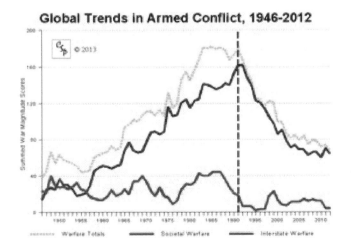

displays showing changes of key indicator measurements over time.

TRENDS MOST LIKELY TO CONTINUE are trends which available evidence indicates are going to continue to follow a specific pattern or direction. For example, if evidence suggests that population growth will continue to increase during the next twenty years, list that trend and suggest the causes and consequences.

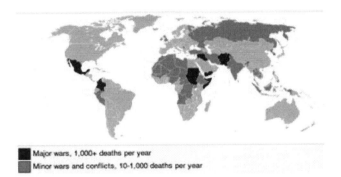

■ Major wars, 1,000+ deaths per year
■ Minor wars and conflicts, 10-1,000 deaths per year

LOCATION AND DISTRIBUTION MAPPING is a method of displaying data about problems, resources, technology, environmental factors, human needs, etc. on maps.

It is crucial that the base map on which data is being displayed is as least-distorted as possible. If the base map is grossly distorted, as most world maps are, then the data being displayed on that map could be distorted and misleading. In addition, the relationships of the data will be distorted; possible solutions will be misleading at best, or masked or exaggerated by the distortion. Maps such as the Mercator world map were valuable inventions in their day (400+ years ago), but in today's globalized world, a more accurate, less distorted view of the whole world is needed.

One such less distorted world map is the Fuller projection (next page).

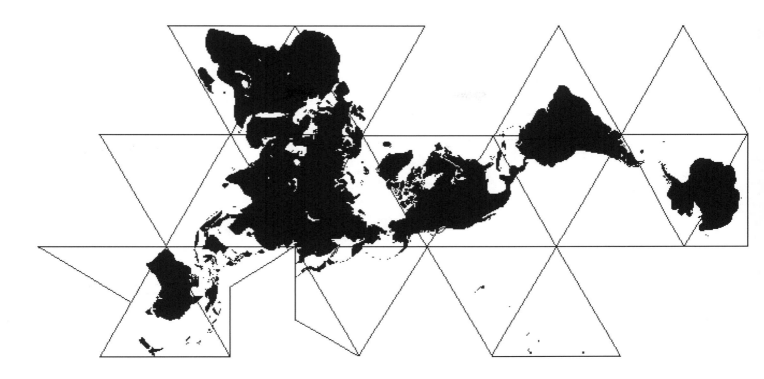

IMPACTS AND INTERACTIONS WITH OTHER AREAS

	Energy	Transportation
Energy	10%	25%
Transportation	30%	1%

CROSS-IMPACT ANALYSIS is a method of analyzing the interactions of different systems or sub-systems such as the analysis is made by constructing a two dimensional matrix with the different systems entered along both dimensions. For example, if you wanted to show the interactions between an energy system and a transportation system, you could construct a matrix with both systems indicated along both dimensions.

You can quantify the matrix by showing how much energy is used by the transportation system, how much transportation is use by the energy system, how much energy is used by the energy system, and how much transportation is used by the transportation system.

The above matrix shows that the energy system under consideration uses 10% of the total available energy to run itself (for mining, transportation, processing, etc.), and 25% of the total transportation system is tied up moving one form or another of energy around (via pipeline, train, truck). The Transportation system uses 30% of the total energy supply (cars, trucks, trains, ships, planes), and 1% of the Transportation system is occupied with moving components of the Transportation system (transporting cars, trucks, parts, etc.).

If you want to know the cross-impacts of an

additional system such as communications or if you want to divide transportation into different subsystems, just list those additions along both dimensions and fill in the new matrix. The quantities you use are your choice and will depend on the types of interactions you want to show. For example, you could use dollars to show money interactions or Kilowatt-hours to show interactions in terms of energy measurement. The interaction matrix can also be used to simply catalogue the interrelationships of different systems, e.g. trucks transport gasoline and gasoline is used to fuel trucks.

DECISION MAKING CRITERIA are the standards by which design and strategic alternatives are evaluated.

AN INVENTION CHART is a chronological list of inventions related to a particular area— such as energy, food, shelter or transportation. An inventions chart is produced by listing, in order of appearance (by year), the inventions or artifacts that influenced the development of the energy, food, etc. system. History helps us understand the context for the present day problems and possible solutions. It helps us see directionality. An inventions chart is a more objective way of seeing history and what is shaping historical choices that humans have.

GLOSSARY is a listing and definition of terms important for understanding the system for which we are designing alternatives. This becomes increasingly

---

Invention Chart Example—Solar Energy

400 BC	Passive solar houses built in the Indus Valley and the U.S. Southwest. Solar heat used for distillation of liquids and drying agricultural products.
200 BC	Greece: Archimedes reportedly concentrates sunlight with reflecting mirrors to set fire to attaching ships.
1700s	Switzerland: de Saussure invents solar flat plate collector and first solar oven.
1860s	France: Meurhot develops 1/2 h.p solar steam engine.
1890s	Chile: Solar distillation plant produces up to 6,000 galleons of water per day
1891	USA: Kemp patents first commercial solar water heater.
1912	Egypt: 50 h.p solar engine pumps irrigation water.
1940s	USA: Basic patents for photovoltaic solar cells.
1950s	France: 50 kw solar furnace built. USA Solar cells available commercially.
1954	USA: silicon photovoltaic cell invented—first solar cell capable of converting enough of the sun's energy into power to run everyday electrical equipment.
1958	USA: First use of solar cells in outer space (Vanguard rocket).
1965	Italy: 100 kw solar tower thermal power plant
1969	France: Large scale mirrored solar furnace produces over 1 MW of power per day at temperatures of 6,000 degrees F.
1974	USA: Mass production of solar cells
1977	France: Electricity for electric grid produced by solar tower energy gererator.
1979	Spain: 50 kw solar farm; USA: 250 kw photovoltaic system used by community college.
1981	USA: 10 MW solar towers begins operation. First solar powered aircraft (flies from France to England)
1982	Australia: first solar powered automobiles.
1986–1999	Solar power plant advancements
2012	China: world's largest solar energy installation with an installed capacity of 200 megawatts.
2013	India: Gujarat Solar Park, a collection of solar farms has a combined installed capacity of 605 megawatts.

relevant for our understanding as well as in later stages of the design science process when we are communicating our strategic designs to the larger system.

RESEARCHERS, AUTHORITIES, AND ORGANIZATIONS

is a listing of individuals and institutions presently engaged in research and development; the people we can contact for feedback or advice on our work; and organizations which influence decisions in different areas related to our design— or who could take our work to the next level, or implement it.

BIBLIOGRAPHY/REFERENCE

is a listing of websites, links, PDFs, books, journals, articles, and other information sources dealing with the design on which we are working.

Group Methods

Your defining and analyzing of the Present, Problem, and Preferred State will generate a series of questions that need to be answered. What/when/where/how/how many, etc, are all likely to come up We need to answer these questions, for in the answers lie potential solutions and the path to the Preferred State.

In our group, ask on of the key questions that needs to be answered. After the question, brainstorm what information sources you would use to find the answer. How would you find the desired information if you couldn't find it through Google or other search engine? What is the ultimate (or primary) source for the data you are seeking? Test the different sources and determine which ones lead to the answer most readily and in which you have the most trust. After running this exercise many times, it is possible to develop a good list of the best sources of data (or sources of sources of data) for use in design science research.

DATA ACQUISITION GAME is a method for learning where to find sources of various data. How it works: Each member of a team asks a question about a specific data point. For example: How many bicycles are there in Australia? How much milk is consumed in Mexico? Where do date palm trees grow? The idea is to stump the other members of the team.

QUESTIONS/EXERCISES

1. Where will you find data for your problem area? How will you organize it?

2. What is an analysis?

3. How will we display or visualize our data? What data visualization techniques will help us understand the larger system and help us find design alternatives?

4. Make an input/output diagram of your house and quantify it.

5. Make a components and processes chart of your house.

6. Make a trend chart showing the number of miles you have traveled per year over the past ten years.

5. Inventory ALTERNATIVES

"If one does not cast a big net, one cannot catch a big fish."

—Chinese Proverb

What choices do we have when we want to design a system that will get us from the Problem State to the Preferred State? And which uses alternatives found in the Present State?

Artifacts/ Alternatives

What artifacts are needed to get us to the Preferred State?

What technological and organizational artifacts are available that will solve the problem/ build the capacity/ realize the Preferred State?

What technology hardware, products, organizational programs, policies, and strategies are needed to reach our Preferred State?

When we are making a plan and we have seen where we are and determined where we want to go, we need to identify all the known alternatives for getting to our goal. It is important that this list be comprehensive so that the range of choices is as inclusive as possible. In order to make as informed a decision as possible we need to be able to compare each alternative to determine which is the best for reaching the Preferred State as quickly as possible for the most number of people using the least amount of resources.

We need to have information about each alternative so that we will be able to know how and where each can be used. We need to know how each alternative works and the particular situations to which each is best suited. Here is a sample form with characteristics of what you might need to know about each alternative:

ALTERNATIVES CHECK LIST

1. What is it? What does it do? How does it do it? How is it used? How do you propose to use it?
2. How does it work?
3. Show/illustrate how it works with diagrams.
4. Where does it come from? What is its history?
5. Capability: What can it produce? At what scale?
6. What resources does it need? How efficient is it?
7. What environmental conditions does it need to operate in?
8. What are its environmental impacts?
9. What resources does it need to operate? What is it made of? What is needed to build or install it?

"I can't understand why people are frightened of new ideas. I'm frightened of the old ones."

—John Cage

10. What are its best uses or applications?
11. What kinds of personnel are needed to install, maintain and run it?
12. How is it managed, regulated, and changed?
13. What are its advantages/benefits? What are the positive impacts—social, economic and ecological?
14. What are the disadvantages/costs? What are the negative impacts—social, economic and ecological?
15. How long will it last? What is its life expectancy/useful life? What happens when its usefulness is over? How will it be recycled?

The availability of alternatives reflects the degree of our freedom of choices. No freedom of choice can exist where there are no alternatives. The more alternatives a system has, the more viable that system will be. Inventorying existing alternatives and *developing new ones* is a critical need of society and the task of the design scientist.

A limited availability of alternatives can threaten the survival of a system. If an electrical circuit has only one pathway for electricity to flow and the wire is broken, the system ceases to function. In an urban electrical grid, as in your brain, there is redundancy. This means

> "We are continually faced with great opportunities which are brilliantly disguised as unsolvable problems."
>
> —Margaret Mead

that if one cable or neuronal circuit breaks or becomes dysfunctional, there are other paths for electricity or signal to flow so that the whole system does not shut down.

Living systems are able to grow in a changing environment because they are incredibly complex, having many alternative pathways for achieving any one goal. Humans are the most complex and adaptable systems so far discovered in nature. For example, it has been estimated by biologists that there are 30,000 pathways for information to flow between any two neurons in our brains.[1] That permits many alternative paths for a signal to move along. We need to employ this principle of redundancy in the design of our preferred system. Alternatives make possible different pathways for achieving the same or similar goals.

QUESTIONS/EXERCISES

1. What is an alternative? What is an inventory of alternatives?
2. What characteristics will we include in our inventory?
3. Where will we find data to do our inventory?
4. Inventory all of the possible methods we could use to conserve energy in our home.

6. Develop EVALUATION CRITERIA

How do we choose the best alternatives?

After all alternatives are inventoried, the next step is to develop a set of evaluation criteria by which each alternative can be assessed. After each alternative is evaluated, the best alternatives can then be selected for our plan.

Evaluation criteria are the guidelines for reaching a Preferred State. They represent our values and priorities. They reflect what we think is important in making decisions about the design, implementation, use and maintenance of systems. Evaluation criteria can be general guidelines for decision makers or they can be performance specifications for the designer. The criteria are developed by formalizing the set of values articulated in the Preferred State. They can first be described qualitatively (general criteria) and then they can be more specifically defined in terms of quantitative measurements. For example, a general criterion for the selection of a transportation system alternative could be that only minimum hydrocarbon or nitrous oxide pollution be permitted. A specific criterion, on the other hand, could indicate the specific amounts of those compounds that are to be permitted. Another general criterion could be that the alternative must convert or use only renewable income energy sources. A specific criterion could specify the range of energy conversion efficiencies necessary for the design of an alternative transportation vehicle.

Pollution control standards could be viewed as evaluation criteria developed to minimize negative environmental impacts of human technology. Since these standards are criteria to measure undesirable substances dispersed in the eco-system, much care has to be taken in determining what are safe levels, in both the short and long-term perspective. Ideally,

the systems you design should have pollution outputs as close to zero as possible. In a regenerative design, an alternative will leave an ecosystem stronger and healthier than before.

The following are general evaluation criteria that have been used by Global Solutions Lab energy teams:

Energy Criteria

EFFICIENCY

- Maximum value placed on doing the most with the least amount of energy
- Minimum use of energy-intensive materials
- Maximum use of reusable materials and packaging
- Minimum energy use in construction, maintenance, and recycling
- Maximum value placed on user's time and energy
- Maximum ease, simplicity, and clarity of repair, replacement, and recycling in minimal time
- Maximum use of modularity of construction where applicable
- Maximum interlinkages of energy-intensive activities
- Maximum use f low impact decentralized energy-harnessing artifacts
- Minimum heat discharge into environment

DIVERSITY

- Minimum dependence on one source of energy
- Maximum diversification and interdependence of energy sources
- Maximum availability and distribution of power
- Maximum comprehensive responsibility and

responsiveness to the needs of energy users by energy suppliers

SAFETY

- Maximum value placed on human life
- Maximum safety in construction, operation, maintenance, and recycling
- Maximum designed-in safety for emergencies and breakdowns
- Maximum safety for future generations

ADAPTABILITY

- Maximum value placed on adaptive stability
- Maximum responsiveness to short-term energy demand changes
- Maximum expandability/contractibility (responsiveness to long-term energy demand changes)
- Maximum reserves of emergency supplies and facilities
- Maximum flexibility and adaptability to new situations

ECOLOGICAL CONTEXT

- Maximum value placed on virgin areas of globe
- Minimum topographical, geological, hydrological, physiographical, limnological, meteorological, soil, vegetation, and wildlife disturbances
- Minimum use of land, water, water space, air, and air space
- Minimum input of solid, liquid, gaseous, and heat waste into ecological context

ORGANIZATION

- Maximum centralization of coordination functions, maximum decentralization of decision-making functions
- Maximum compatibility between different energy systems, and levels of energy systems. Energy production systems for use by single families, schools, health units, etc., should be compatible and able to work with large scale utility-level systems

USER CRITERIA

- Maximum value placed on meeting energy needs of 100% of humanity; *sufficiency*—enough energy for everyone; *accessibility*—distribution to everyone
- Maximum *quality control* of energy artifact, system, or service
- Maximum *reliability* of energy artifact, system, or service; maximum use of back-up systems to further increased reliability
- Maximum *durability* of energy artifact, system, or service
- Maximum ease, *simplicity,* and clarity of use of energy artifact, system, or service
- Maximum *stability* and *consistency* of output of energy artifact, system, or service
- Maximum cultural, esthetic, and individual human option *diversity*
- Maximum *decentralization* of information flow
- Maximum use of *feedback*
- Maximum *knowledge* about energy system interactions with all other systems, especially the ecological context

QUESTIONS/EXERCISES

1. What is an evaluation?

2. What are criteria?

3. What kinds of criteria will you include in order to choose from your inventory of alternatives?

4. What criteria would you use if you were going to design your own house?

5. What criteria do you use in selecting the food you eat?

7. DESIGN the Preferred System

"You never change things by fighting the existing reality. To change something, build a new model that makes the existing model obsolete."

—R. Buckminster Fuller

Strategy Development: How, how, how?

What would your preferred system look like? What does it do? How does it work? And, how does *that* work? What are the results and impacts it has? What are its parts?

Designing the preferred system is where we construct a detailed plan or blueprint of your ideal system. The plan is an organization or description of related elements that, if implemented, could get us to the Preferred State. This is where the proverbial rubber hits the road.

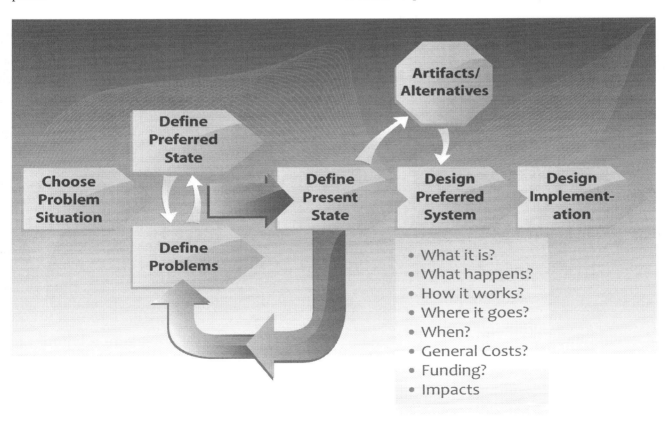

- What it is?
- What happens?
- How it works?
- Where it goes?
- When?
- General Costs?
- Funding?
- Impacts

We design the preferred system by:

1. Considering the values, goals and measurable targets expressed in the Preferred State.
2. Selecting the alternative(s) that will get us to the Preferred State, while also being in tune with our values (Decision Making Criteria).
3. Integrating the alternatives we have selected into a coordinated system.
4. Fitting the design into a timeframe for its implementation.

Selecting the appropriate alternative elements and integrating them into a solution that gets us to the Preferred State involves several steps:

1. Determine which of the alternatives in our inventory gets us to the Preferred State, and meet the requirements or specifications of our evaluation criteria.
2. Examine the relevant environmental conditions of the geographic area (global, regional, local) for which we are planning. For example, if we are designing an energy system, we might list solar intensity, precipitation, ecosystem types, natural available resources, average daily wind velocity, etc.
3. Determine which of the alternatives are appropriate to our plan by matching the Preferred State needs and environmental conditions required by each to the existing conditions of the areas on which we are focusing. For example, a wind-powered generator would be appropriate in a mildly windy area while a solar collector would be inappropriate in an area that receives very little solar radiation. If it is apparent that there are few, if any, appropriate alternatives that would contribute to the resolution of the problem, we need to develop a set of performance characteristics for several ideal alternatives.

These criteria can then be used by a design team for development of new alternatives and artifacts.

4. Integrate the appropriate alternatives into a working system where all of the parts are functionally interconnected and coordinated. This step usually involves experimenting with different contributions of alternatives until a workable and optimal solution is achieved.

Efficiently running systems can have parts that if tested separately would perform inefficiently. (This understanding is implicit in the definition of synergy: the behavior of a system unpredicted by the sum of its parts. Another way of looking at synergy: a chain is as strong as the total interaction of its links, not as would be expected—that of its weakest link.) The implications of this phenomena for solution design is that we need to remember that we are designing a 'whole system'— and it is the behavior and performance of *that* system on which we need to focus, not its parts.

When we are organizing our preferred system, consider the following factors:

1. How will the system operate and function?
2. What impacts will it have— both intended and positive, and unintended and negative?
3. How will the system be built, installed, managed, and regulated? Who will do this?
4. How will the system differ from the present system?
5. How will the system be monitored so that evaluation of its performance could be made? How can it be improved?
6. How will the system increase the personal freedoms and number of learning opportunities for people?
7. How will the system adapt to further technological innovations and social change?

8. How will the system be used by a wide range of cultural systems?

The preferred system can be described with many of the same tools you used to describe the Present State. For example, you might develop an *Input/Output diagram* showing the flows of energy, materials, information and people through the system. You will also want to diagram the *Components and Processes* of the different parts and processes of the system. *Trend charts* could be developed to show how such a system would contribute to the conservation of natural resources and/or increase the levels of adequate distribution of essential goods and services.

Following your original intentions, the plan should emphasize the level of aggregation (global, regional, community or single dwelling unit for example) that you chose to focus on, but it should also describe the interrelationships of similar functional systems at other levels of aggregation. For example, a community food system could be related to the regional and global food systems or vice versa. Showing how your strategic design could scale— be replicated en mass— is also important for showing the global impacts of your strategy.

A design science plan should be grounded in our vision of an achievable Preferred State, not a speculative fantasy. It needs to show how, using present day technology and resources we can achieve the Preferred State. Our Preferred State, and the plan for reaching it should not be confined to present modes of thinking, political constraints or projections of what is likely to happen. It should be based on what we want to *make* happen and out explicit design for making real our preferred vision.

Design science deals with what is technologically possible but not necessarily with what is politically probable. The primary constraints on the plan are technological (is it possible given current know- how?) and ecological (is it compatible with natural systems? Can it be implemented, minimally, without ecological damage? And optimally, can its implementation help regenerate ecological systems?). A plan uses what is currently available in resources, technology, and know-how. For example, nuclear fusion could not be included in an energy plan because fusion is presently not a technologically feasible energy option. (It could also have a number of other characteristics that are counter to our evaluation criteria.)

A design science strategic design is based on what we want and what is possible. It shows how a system could be organized to fulfill our preferred values and goals. It is real to the extent that we can organize ourselves and the environment to realize the plan. In some ways, this planning stage can be likened to what an architect does in designing and specifying the elements of a new building or system of buildings. Resources, needs, wants, potentials, and constraints are all integrated into an image—a blueprint—of a preferred system. This part of the design science process is the development of our "blueprint."

Gap Analysis

Once you have a Preferred State and the Problem State defined, you can quantify the gap between the two. For example, if the Preferred State is everyone in the world having access to electricity, and the Problem State is that 1 billion people are without access, then the gap is 1 billion people. This "gap analysis" is a useful tool for measuring what your solution and its strategy for implementation need to accomplish, the resources it will need, its cost, and benefits.

What makes a *compelling* design and plan?

1. Our Preferred State is compelling.
2. Our design gets us to the Preferred State.
3. Our design gets to the Preferred State with present day technology.
4. Our design gets to the Preferred State with known resources.
5. Our design and implementation are "affordable." The more affordable the better.
6. Our design and implementation are "affordable." The more affordable the better. The more profitable, the better. The more people who "win," the better.
7. The more understandable our design, the better.
8. The more sustainable our design, the more people positively impacted by our design, the better.
9. What else?

QUESTIONS

1. What is a plan?
2. What is a model?
3. What levels of aggregation are we going to design for?
4. What technologies are you going to use in your plan?
5. What geographic, climatic, and ecological conditions are you designing for?

EXERCISES

1. Design your diet for the next week:
    a. What foods will you eat?
    b. What is their nutritional content?
    c. Where will you get the food?
    d. What tools will you need to prepare the food?
2. Make a plan of a house you would like to live in and consider the following functions:
    a. Energy sources and use
    b. Water and waste systems
    c. Food preparation and storage
    d. Lighting
    e. Space configuration
    f. Materials
    g. Construction tools
    h. Structure of enclosure

Wind

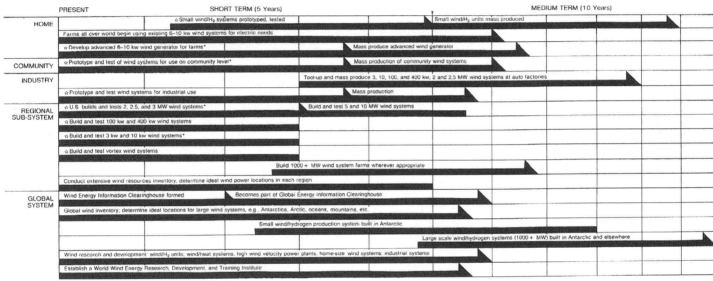

	PRESENT	SHORT TERM (5 Years)	MEDIUM TERM (10 Years)

HOME
- ☆ Small wind/H₂ systems prototyped, tested → Small wind/H₂ units mass produced
- Farms all over world begin using existing 6–10 kw wind systems for electric needs
- ☆ Develop advanced 6–10 kw wind generator for farms* → Mass produce advanced wind generator

COMMUNITY
- ☆ Prototype and test of wind systems for use on community level* → Mass production of community wind systems

INDUSTRY
- Tool-up and mass produce 3, 10, 100, and 400 kw, 2 and 2.5 MW wind systems at auto factories
- ☆ Prototype and test wind systems for industrial use → Mass production

REGIONAL SUB-SYSTEM
- ☆ U.S. builds and tests 2, 2.5, and 3 MW wind systems* → Build and test 5 and 10 MW wind systems
- ☆ Build and test 100 kw and 400 kw wind systems
- ☆ Build and test 3 kw and 10 kw wind systems*
- ☆ Build and test vortex wind systems
- Build 1000 + MW wind system farms wherever appropriate
- Conduct extensive wind resources inventory, determine ideal wind power locations in each region

GLOBAL SYSTEM
- Wind Energy Information Clearinghouse formed → Becomes part of Global Energy Information Clearinghouse
- Global wind inventory; determine ideal locations for large wind systems, e.g., Antarctica, Arctic, oceans, mountains, etc.
- Small wind/hydrogen production system built in Antarctic
- Large scale wind/hydrogen systems (1000 + MW) built in Antarctic and elsewhere
- Wind research and development: wind/H₂ units; wind/heat systems; high wind velocity power plants; home-size wind systems; industrial systems
- Establish a World Wind Energy Research, Development, and Training Institute

*Currently underway   ☆ Artifact

8. IMPLEMENTATION

Strategy development: How, how, how?

Once we have designed the plan for reaching our preferred system, the next questions to be resolved are:

- How do you get from here to there—from the Present to the Preferred State?
- What stages and levels of implementation do we have to consider? A strategy is an arrangement of all the steps that must be completed along a time line showing the order in which they must be done. At the left end of the time line below is the present problem and at the right is the proposed future. Along the time line will be the "things which need to be done" to get to the Preferred State.

In developing a complex strategy, it may become clear that all of the steps cannot be included on a single time line. In this situation we need to divide the strategy into a number of time lines. These lines can be either parallel or overlapping. There are two major ways of dividing a strategy. The first is to separate the implementation steps into different aggregate levels such as single dwelling unit, neighborhood, community, region and global. The next breakdown is to further subdivide

Implementation

- What we do
- What we need to do it
- How we do it
- Who does it
- When (1st 6 months)
- When (1st year, etc.)
- Costs, to who
- Funding, from where
- Results

each of these levels in terms of the different functional areas. For example, you might want to divide the implementation steps of a regional food system into the following subsystems: production, transportation, processing, storage, distribution, consumption, waste recycling, etc.

The chart on the previous page is an example of a sub-strategy of a global energy development plan proposed in *Energy, Earth and Everyone.*[2] The development of wind power is described at different aggregate levels along a ten year time line.

After the total implementation period has been determined comes the question: Wwhat stages of development must occur at what point during the overall implementation period? This kind of scheduling is "determining first things first" or critical path planning. For example, a hydrogen-powered transport vehicle has to be prototyped, tested, and proven feasible before a transportation using this vehicle can be designed and implemented.

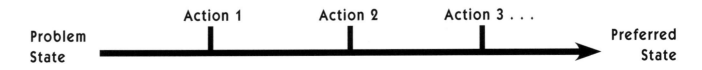

Problem State ——— Action 1 ——— Action 2 ——— Action 3 . . . ———▶ Preferred State

A design science strategy is a logical sequence of events that shows how, starting from present conditions, a future Preferred State can be achieved. A strategy is the "bridge" from the present "problem" state to the future "preferred" state.

A design science strategy needs to also address the following:

1. Who will implement the strategy?
2. How can these people and groups be invited to participate or be mobilized?
3. What tools and artifacts will be needed to implement the strategy?
4. How, when and by whom can those tools and artifacts be produced and distributed?
5. How can the strategy be evaluated and improved?
6. How can the various groups of people who will benefit or be impacted by our strategy support and participate in the implementation of the strategy, or a part of our strategy? This important step should be further developed at this point. Increasing the awareness and participation among those people who will be affected by the plan could be integrated into the entire process from beginning to end. For example, illustrating the benefits of alternatives to the present non-Preferred State system will increase receptivity to our design.

There is a proposal in *Energy Earth and Everyone* to create a Global Energy Utility that would be charged with the responsibility for developing global energy sources and systems located in the global commons, or outside of any single nations jurisdiction. The intention of this strategy is not to show what will happen, but what can happen over time if scheduled steps of development are implemented.

The more comprehensive and anticipatory a strategy, the better its chances of effecting the most positive change for humanity. In developing a comprehensive strategy, all the variables that affect the attainment of the strategy should be taken into account. In defining the problem, these variables are explored for their effect on the problem, and when the solution is defined, the comprehensive strategy describes the implementation of the solution.

QUESTIONS

1. What is a strategy?
2. What are stages of implementation?
3. How long will each stage of implementation take?
4. What industries and commercial services are involved in this strategy? Who would implement the strategy if you had the necessary finances?
5. Who are the users or consumers of the plan?
6. Who are the decision-makers that will be involved? When will they become involved?

9. DOCUMENT **THE PROCESS**

During every step in the design science planning process it is important to record our research progress and group sessions. This documentation provides the raw material to produce a report when our work is at this stage. While the objective of our group may not be to publish and distribute a finished foundation proposal, business plan or document at this time, recording the progress of the work is often the best way to "store" the generated information for future referral.

The Global Solutions Lab uses an online wiki that documents its progress[3]. The wiki is set up as a series of questions, the answers to which are the design science strategic design and plan. You will find these questions in the Appendix.

The goal of the documentation process is to have what amounts to a business plan or foundation proposal for investment or funding for the next stages of the design science process. Such a document needs to

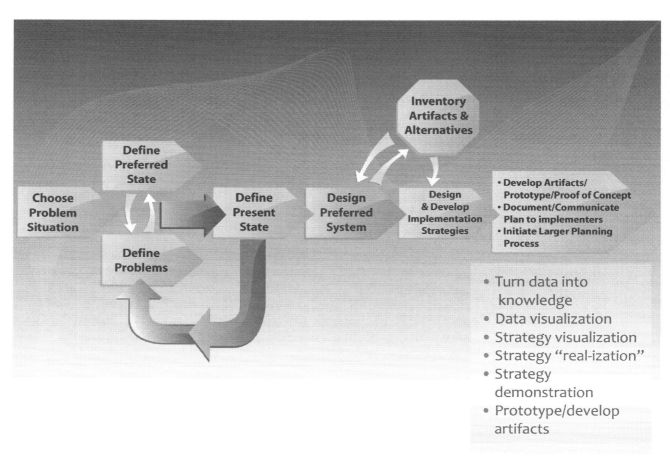

show, among other things, the need, what our strategy will do, and how much it will cost. This recognizes the fact that there are not many people who are in a position to self-finance the development of a strategic design. At some point, the design scientist will likely need to seek resources that go beyond his or her financial wherewithal. Where this point is, is dependent on what the overall strategy is, what artifact(s) are necessary to be developed and tested, the resources of the design scientist, and other factors.

The documentation stage is crucial to the entire process. Whether it is a business plan, foundation proposal, crowd-funding proposal, policy white paper, journal article or all the above, the design scientist needs to be able to communicate their work to the larger system (that of society, investors, etc.) so that the strategic design gets implemented. It does no one any good to have a brilliant strategy that can improve the world sitting on the shelf gathering dust.

The work that you produce will likely be useful to other groups that follow. The more thoroughly the entire process is documented the more valuable the report will be to you and to other groups.

Design science teams need to document their work using all or a combination of the following tools:

- Research reports
- Bibliographies
- Charts/graphs
- Drawings
- On-line presentations, TED Talks, YouTube presentations
- Physical models
- Photography
- Power Points
- Web sites

QUESTIONS/EXERCISES

1. List different ways you can document your work. Decide which methods you will use.
2. How would you do a YouTube that documents your design science strategy?
3. How would you design an exhibit of your plan?
4. Write a research report on an alternative you have investigated.
5. Write a report on the values and goals your group generated and how you came to agree on a shared set of goals.

10. Take the INITIATIVE

"The design scientist undertakes fundamental invention, self-underwriting, development and experimental proof of inventions, as demonstrated for instance by the Wright Brothers, wherein the design science professional will be equipped with all the economic, legal and technological knowledge necessary for reducing such inventions to on-going industrial practice."

—Buckminster Fuller

Initiative springs
Only from within
The individual.
Initiative can neither
Be created nor delegated
It can only be vacated.
Initiative can only
Be taken by the
Individual on his
Own self-conviction

Of the necessity
To overcome his
Conditioned reflexing
Which has accustomed
Him heretofore
Always to yield authority
To the wisdom
Of others. Initiative
Is only innate
And highly perishable.

—Buckminster Fuller

What do I do with the plan?

How can I implement it?

How can I bring about a positive change in the world?

Up to this point we have discussed the step by step method by which we can determine what needs to be done and how. Now comes the steps needed to start the implementation of the plan.

There are three ways for us to further develop our work and to help bring about positive change. We can:

1. Develop the tools or artifacts called for by the design science strategy we have formulated (if they don't already exist). And if they do exist, in part or whole, we can test them out in the configuration(s) we have designed to see if our design works as we intend.

2. Communicate the plan to those who would be involved, affected, or interested in getting involved as a business proposition or investment, or because the initiative matches their values and what they want to do.

3. Initiate a larger planning process that includes seeking the participation of those who would be involved in implementing, funding or benefitting from the plan; or all three can be undertaken concurrently.

Developing The Artifact

The design science process provides us with a rationale and a frame of reference for what is needed. *"What is needed"* can often be translated into a physical or "metaphysical" *artifact.*

This is the first and primary output of the design science process. Since the implementation of our strategic design/plan will require developing artifacts that may not have yet been invented, tested, or configured in the manner which we are proposing, we need to compile a list of the artifacts that need to be "invented" (or put together) to make our strategic design real. Along with the artifact, we need to state the specifications for its performance— what it is to accomplish. These performance specifications (or design criteria), are specific guidelines for what the artifact is supposed to do in terms of impacts and intended consequences, materials and energy usage, safety, performance, ecological impact, efficiency and adaptability.

The global design science strategy formulated in the book *Energy, Earth and Everyone* defines the need to harness the Earth's income energy sources. After studying the energy flows and concentrations through the whole Earth system, the winds of Antarctica were seen as a potential source of energy. Because of the unique and intense conditions in Antarctica, a special artifact is needed to harness these winds. Most windmills build to date have been primarily designed to harness low intensity winds of the planet—winds blowing from 7 to 25 mph. Winds below or above these limits result in either no power or damage to the windmill. Winds in parts of Antarctica average over 28 mph for 340 days per year and often exceed 100 mph. To harness these winds, a wind turbine specifically designed for high-speed winds is needed.

Once an artifact—in this case a wind turbine capable of functioning in the Antarctic—has been identified, it can be built, tested, refined, and then utilized to meet the stated need. Designing, building, and testing the artifact involves a specific design science process.

The process is a systematic outline for designing an artifact.

In the chart on the next page, the box in the lower left, *Artifact Development*, is the area where the idea for the artifact is developed into a design and workable prototype. This first prototype is tested and refined into Prototypes 2 and 3. As preparation for this stage, the design scientist first searches for related or similar designs. If similar work has already been done, there is no reason to repeat it. We can learn from and build on it.

In terms of the Antarctic wind energy source example, we need to see if there is already a high strength windmill or a design for one that be adapted. In addition, helicopter rotor design and construction, tower design and construction, specific weather and geographical conditions in Antarctica (where is the best spot for a forest of windmills in the Antarctic from the point of view of the wind, from the point of view of construction and logistics), materials science (which materials are best suited to the Antarctic extremes), local and remote companies, agencies and authorities in the field who we can contact are all important to find out about.

The next step, after all the relevant information has been gathered, organized, and integrated, is to begin the actual design. A first prototype is built. If parts for the artifact are available, they are integrated into the desired unit. If apparatus is not available, then we need to begin to fabricate the artifact from "scratch." What we are able to do ourself is dependent on our unique background, training, inclinations and the demands of the design. What we can't do ourself, we need to bring in collaborators, partners and/or investors for so we can hire the relevant expertise and skill sets to build and test our prototype.

The design scientist is often a synthesizer, an integrator of already existing parts into new synergetic arrangements. Obviously, an individual cannot mine, refine and alloy the various metals needed for a windmill, nor should he or she be expected to have all the skills necessary to reduce a complex idea to a physical artifact. The design scientist needs to be skilled in knowing how to get anything that needs to be done, done. This entails knowing who can do what, and

Design Science Process: Artifact Development

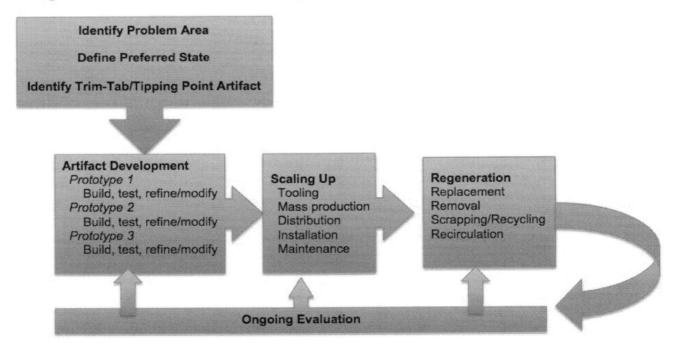

where, when, and how. One very beneficial side effect of this process is that the design scientist can obtain a comprehensive education by following his or her idea through to completion. Many skills and talents are brought into focus at one time or another in the process of reducing an idea to ongoing industrial practice.

Once the first prototype is built, it is then tested and refined into a second prototype. It is usually necessary to repeat this cycle of prototyping, testing, and refining an average of three times to work out all the bugs in a design. The third prototype should fulfill the performance specifications set out in the beginning stage, or those specified after more information has been gathered.

The prototyping of an idea, and the subsequent testing of that idea as a physical (or policy) artifact to see whether it is indeed a viable alternative can be done by an individual or group. The next stage, if the strategic design calls for a physical artifact, is the actual industrial manufacture of the working prototype, the production design, tooling, production, and subsequent distribution, installation, maintenance, and service. Because these steps usually require more resources than an individual or small group could bring to bear, the active support of a much larger group, the other two outputs of the design science process, "communicating the plan" and "initiating a larger planning process" enter the picture.

COMMUNICATING THE PLAN

This refers to the documentation and communication of the work done in the design science planning process. It includes the basic information and context of what the problem is, what the Preferred State is, the alternatives, the strategy, etc. This documentation is put together as a business plan, foundation proposal or report that can be sent out to others in the field and related individuals, groups, corporations, organizations, and

government agencies that were identified in the course of the planning process for evaluative feedback. A new document which incorporates this feedback is written and distributed to the public. This documentation stage is a very important step in the design science process.

Science is a collective effort in which current investigators are indebted to those who have come before. It is very important that any design science experiment or testing of a hypothesis (e.g. can humanity feed itself on a regenerative basis?) be recorded so that others who will carry the work further or in different directions can profit from the work.

INITIATING A LARGER PLANNING PROCESS

This store is related to the preceding outputs of the design science process in two ways. As it has already been pointed out, reducing a design idea to an industrially produced artifact may involve more resources and skills than the individual or team possess. The strategy needs to be communicated to those who have the necessary industrial resources and capabilities to implement the strategic design and plan. We have identified who these individuals, groups, organizations and corporations are in the initial search phase of the design science process.

The second way in which initiating a larger planning process relates to the other outputs is in furthering the implementation of the larger developmental strategy of which the artifact is only one part. In all planning it is crucial to involve the people who will benefit or be impacted by a particular plan. The purpose of a design science plan or strategy is primarily the testing of a hypothesis and the development of alternatives rather than planning for others. Once a new option or alternative has been developed it can then be widely disseminated and a larger planning process instituted.

In this later process, those who the strategy would

effect can become involved in the process. To a degree, this will be similar to the effort that the individual design scientist or small group has already gone through. In no way is this a meaningless exercise: The people who will be effected by the plan need to know, need to find out for themselves (and not be told by "experts"), just what are their collective goals and what are the limitations and possibilities of their specific situation. People should plan, not "be planned for" because one of the most beneficial aspects of planning is the educational process which takes place during the actual planning. Beyond this, for any complex development plan to succeed, it needs the full understanding and active participation of all the people involved in the plan.

As stated before, the ultimate goal of the design science process is to bring about constructive change. It is to allow everyone on Earth the option of being a "have" rather than a "have not." Sub-goals, or steps, along the way to this overall goal include the generation and testing of new options for humanity, the development of detailed strategies for the realization of new artifacts that are needed for a strategy, the initiation of a larger planning process, and the self-education of the design scientist.

Design Science Process Summary

An artifact that is needed for a strategic design and plan's realization is prototyped and tested, then mass produced and distributed, maintained, replaced, and recycled when there is an improved item available. This strategy is documented, made widely available and feedback elicited. Where appropriate, a local planning process is instituted in the specific areas where the strategic design and plan has furnished new alternatives and can, when implemented, reach the Preferred State.

It should be understood that goals are revised, clarified and restated and that what design science seeks to do is re-define goals, create new options and solve real-world problems.

Design science involves a long-range perspective which includes the knowledge that everything has its own gestation rates. For a human baby, it is 9 months, for an elephant it is 21 months, for an artifact or comprehensive design strategy it is usually considerably longer. As in any long distance voyage, periodical navigational fixes are taken and subsequent course corrections are made in order to "stay on course." The same applies to the long-range goals of design science. New information will alter the existing information; as goals are approached, they take on greater clarity and possible new goals emerge.

Conclusions and Next Steps

"The world is in a race between education and catastrophe."

— H. G. Wells

The *Design Science Primer* is intended, as stated in Part 1, to provide a set of tools for changing the world. It is intended to provide perspective and a methodology for participating in the solution of problems that will help the world meet our needs using available technology (or inventing new alternatives), for winning that race between education and catastrophe.

Hope is where values and vision meet the future. The *Primer* has sought to foster hope as it provides techniques for transforming vision into hope made real. It seeks to channel and organize imagination and science to develop innovative and viable solutions to critical real-world problems. Its success will be meassured by what we do with the informatiion contained in this document.

QUESTIONS/EXERCISES

1. What is initiative?
2. What initiatives could your group take to further the development of your plan?
3. What initiative could you take?
4. How would you communicate your plan?
5. What artifacts could you or your group develop?
6. Make a list of experts or authorities you would like to submit your plan to for feedback.
7. Who would you contact if you wanted to initiate a larger planning process?
8. What specialists would you need to assist you in developing the artifact you have chosen?

APPENDIX

The Global Solutions Lab/design science wiki is organized as a series of questions. The answers to these questions will be the first draft of a design science strategic design and plan.

Topic/Issue/Problem area

- The general human need area our team is focusing on is . . .
- The specific problem situation we are working on is . . .

Preferred State

- The Preferred State for the global problem situations we have picked to work on is . . .

Problem State/Present State

- The global problem state for (our problem area) is . . .
- The symptoms of this problem are . . .
- The quantitative description of the problem is . . . (how many of what, etc.)
- The severity of the problem can be measured by . . .
- What are the implications of the problem—how does it impact other areas and systems?
- What are its interconnections with other problems? (This problem impacts the food [shelter, health, education, transportation, economic, environmental] system in the following ways:
- What does the problem look like? (What image(s) describe the problem situation?)
- How many people does the problem impact in the world? Where is it most severe?
- It is most severe in . . .
- What does the geographical dimension look like?

Preferred State

- The Preferred State for the (problem area/situation) we are working on is . . .
    - o *By 2016:*
    - o *By 2030:*
- What will the world (or region we are focused on) look life if this problem is solved?
- If this problem is solved . . .
- How will we measure success? How will we know when we reach the Preferred State?
- We will know we have achieved the Preferred State when . . .
- We will reach this Preferred State in the year 2____.

Present State

- The Problem State is a part of the Present State. What does the Present State look like?
- What are the components and processes of the Present State?
- What are the inputs and outputs of the Present State?

Alternatives

- We know where we are and where we want to go. What are the options for reaching the Preferred State?
  - What present-day technology or policies can be used that will get us to the Preferred State?
  - What artifacts, if scaled up/mass produced/disseminated could get us to the Preferred State?
  - What present day technology can be scaled up to have the impact needed to reach the Preferred State?
- What could you get a patent on?

'Plan'

- What do we do/what needs to happen to reach the Preferred State?
  - To reach the Preferred State we need to ...

Plan—Artifacts

- What artifacts will the plan use to reach the Preferred State?
  - The strategy will use the following artifacts to reach the Preferred State ...
  - How many?
- What is the proof of concept (what is needed to justify scaling up)?

Plan—Timeline

- What do we do in the next six months to reach the Preferred State?
  - In the next six months we will ...
  - What needs to be done over the next five years?

Plan—Impacts

- What impacts will this strategy have on other areas?
- What are the expected and measurable outcomes of this strategy?

Plan—Resources

- What resources does this plan need?
    - The strategy needs the following material resources:
    - The strategy needs the following human resources (Who will implement the strategy? Who is needed for the strategy's success?)
- Where are they? How do we get them?
- What technology is needed? How do we get it?

Plan—Cost

- How much will our strategy cost?
    - The strategy will cost approximately . . .
- Where will this money come from/how will this strategy be financed?
    - The money will come from ...

Plan—Who can do it?

- What can the UN do to make this strategy real?
- What can civil society do?
- What can business do?
- What can individuals do?

Plan—You

- What can I do to make this strategy real?
    - I can . . .
- What can I do to make this strategy real?
- What could I do with $100,000 to move this strategy to the next level?
    - With $100,000 I would ...

ENDNOTES

1   Neuroscience of the Brain, Heidelberg University. http://www.uni-heidelberg.de/md/izn/teaching/neuroscience/img/neuroscience-of-the-brain-english.pdf
2   *Energy, Earth and Everyone*, Medard Gabel, Anchor Press/Doubleday, 1980.
3   wiki.designsciencelab.com

21030737R00058

Made in the USA
Middletown, DE
17 June 2015